Awake Ethics

Awake Ethics

A system for aligning your actions with your core intentions

Written and Illustrated by

Hilary Jane Grosskopf

Contents

I am a fountain, You are my water.
I flow from You to You.

I am an eye, You are my light,
I look from You to You.

You are neither my right nor my left.
You are my foot and my arm as well.

I am a traveler, You are my road.
I go from You to You.

- Zeynep Hatun

Preface

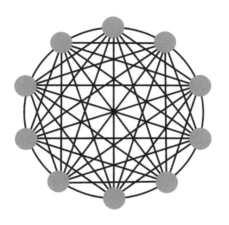

Preface to Awake Ethics

In my experience as a leader and as an active participant in the world of business, I have been surprised at the persistent prevalence of issues such as lack of trust, acknowledgement, opportunity, and ownership in modern organizations. Some ethical issues such as privacy and harassment make it into the media spotlight but many go unacknowledged and unresolved. They build up and eventually cause health issues and unnecessary, unfortunate losses for organizations. My quest began with the questions: Why do ethical issues persist, really? Is there a sustainable solution?

Ethics were not something that I studied in depth in school or have been particularly interested in throughout my life. I took one business ethics class in school and I found it confusing that there were so many contradicting views on what are "right" and "wrong" approaches to human behavior, interactions, and decisions in business. The professor kept coming around to the same conclusions as to what was ethical in a given situation: it depends. Once I became a leader in the business realm, I found that profit-centered progress and human-centered progress often don't quite agree or align. An action can be good for the goal of profit but not so good for the goal of human connection, peace, and development.

I studied many systems and approaches to leadership early on in my career. A particular system of ethics resonated and was so applicable to my leadership at work. After more study and experience as a leader in the field, I found that this system, when viewed through a modern lens and applied to my leadership, did indeed help positively direct my attention, mindset, and interactions day-to-day. I enjoyed satisfying progress. I felt less stressed and more connected. I led my team toward new potential beyond just civility and status quo work. We enjoyed our work more and made progress toward our objectives with more ease and enthusiasm. I found that creative leaders can drive profitable progress with human-centered decision-making. This system was crucial for retaining the best team members and making optimal progress. This is the system and approach I share with you in this book.

As leaders, we have a choice as to how to communicate and engage with others. We have a choice about how to show up in the world and the impact we make. We shape our own journey step by step, interaction by interaction, decision by decision. We also shape the journey of others we interact with. Leaders have power and responsibility over their own journey as well as the journey of their team members. I believe that it is especially important for rising leaders to study ethics in practice and understand how certain key, universal ethical guidelines can improve the way we collaborate and lead.

I'm excited to share Awake Ethics because the principles underscore the deeper purpose of collaboration and the point of companies and organizations that get so cluttered and twisted in our highly commercialized and incentivized world of business. This guidebook is written for rising leaders seeking to make genuine connections with others, learn, and reach their highest potential. It is for leaders seeking to find true alignment and balance of human-centered progress and profit-centered progress. This universal system of ethics can completely change how you collaborate with others, how confident you feel at work, and how you move along your authentic path. The ten ethical principles will help you navigate though ethical decisions with more confidence and collaborate with more joy and ease. They will be like secret agent tools to add to your tool belt on this journey toward your highest potential as a leader in your work and your life.

I hope you find this system of ethics thought-provoking and applicable in your own leadership. I encourage you to also come to your own conclusions as to what ethics really are and what "the most good" really is. I hope that Awake Ethics allows you to deepen your experience and the experience of your team in positive ways that you may not have thought possible... Enjoy the process... and the results.

xo Hilary

Introduction

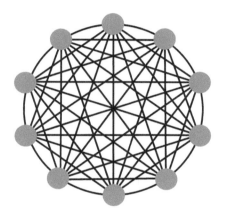

Leadership and Ethics

Unlike the popular term **leadership**, the term **ethics** is not a buzzword used very often in companies and organizations. Many companies have a set of values and basic guidelines but few focus on ethics. Ethics is definitely not a sexy word and many people think ethics are just for troublemakers to learn. It's assumed that we're all ethical as professionals, so little time is spent on learning what ethics are and why they're important.

Ethics became important to me once I was working in the field as a leader and really saw in action, through experience, how interpersonal conflict and obstacles inhibited individuals, teams, and whole organizations from reaching their objectives. I also saw how ethics could go beyond just setting a basic standard for interpersonal civility, to really enable progress and transformation. By practicing ten simple principles, based on an ancient system of ethical conduct, I found that organizations can be environments where teams work harmoniously and enthusiastically while still remaining productive and efficient. Throughout the book, I'll detail how the ten principles, when put into practice, enable organizations to grow and thrive, while allowing people at the individual level to feel supported and challenged as well.

Before we dive into the ten principles and the guidebook work, let's look a bit more closely at what ethics really are and why we should care about leadership ethics.

What are Ethics, really?

Ethics are traditionally defined as principles or guidelines for moral behavior that adhere to the standards our society accepts. They are guiding principles for our behavior; how we should act towards each other and ourselves in ways that cultivate peace and civility. Ethics sound simple enough but in practice, especially in the complex and often competitive environment of business, it can be difficult to really know what is the most ethical action to take and why. Have you found this to be true?

There are many misperceptions of ethics. Many believe that if someone is brought up by good people, they are naturally ethical, conduct themselves appropriately in the workplace, and collaborate elegantly. Another misperception is that as someone gains life experience, they naturally develop ethical behavior. Many people think ethics and values are the same thing. Values and ethics are not the same. Values are qualities that are desirable, or qualities to aspire to. Values are much more subjective than ethics. When companies just have values, they're skipping over ethics. Finally, ethics and etiquette are also very different. Etiquette is a code of conduct that is only relevant for a specific society or group at specific time period. Rules of etiquette stem from a more basic, universal ethical foundation.

Ethics are timeless principles for human conduct, based on a universal understanding, that translate to specific actions. When we study ethics, we begin at the root level of the action: the why and the how. Ethics are therefore decision-making tools, since each action we take is really a decision we make upstream from the action. Let's move on to talk about why a system of ethics is relevant and important for rising leaders.

Why Practice Leadership Ethics?

During my experience in the business world, I found that ethical issues and misunderstandings are the most common obstacles to peace and progress. A shared understanding of ethics was missing. Ethical alignment makes or breaks the culture of a team or organization. A lack of alignment around universal ethical intentions and language results in confusion and interpersonal conflict. I have found that, at any given point in time, teams and organizations fall into one of four categories.

	Not Peaceful	**Peaceful**
Progressing	**Category C** ✓ Progressing	**Category A** ✓ Peaceful ✓ Progressing
Not Progressing	**Category D**	**Category B** ✓ Peaceful

Clearly, the objective of any organization, team, or individual is to be in Category A: peaceful and progressing. There are a few exceptions where Category B or C may be desirable for a specific time or phase of the team's evolution. However, B and C are not sustainable for teams of rising leaders and growing organizations. Let's look at why.

Peace means civility and harmony in interactions. Peace leads to a sustainable day-to-day work environment, free of drama and interpersonal conflict. Peace sets the stage for collaboration. Interpersonal drama, conflict, and misunderstandings are major obstacles to collaboration and the success of the team. This lack of basic human civility and understanding causes the founders and top-level leadership to get involved in peace-making. An environment of peacefulness, through support and alignment, is the first beneficial result of the Awake Ethics system.

However, for growing companies and rising leaders, a system of ethics that provides peace and civility is not adequate. Though this peaceful foundation is important for collaboration to take place, growing companies cannot be satisfied with just civility. Rising leaders and growing businesses need to progress and evolve. Also, financial profit is necessary in business. Sometimes the objective is clear, the resources are available, and the team is ready but lack of motivation and enthusiasm is a deterrent to constructive, focused progress. The second result of the Awake Ethics system is engagement and enthusiasm (or what we could even call happiness). Engagement and enthusiasm fuel progress. Peace and progress enable organizations, teams, and individuals to grow and transform sustainably. Category A teams drive profit from a primary intention of human-centered progress and therefore efficiently and enthusiastically move toward their highest potential through human-centered actions.

Category B teams are usually found within larger organizations. These teams are peaceful and sustaining day-to-day but are often stagnant. This category is stable and may be desirable if you're looking for consistency. However, for rising leaders and achievers, this category can lead to a lack of peacefulness because a lack of progress means a lack of learning and transformational, challenging opportunities.

Category C teams are commonly found in start-ups. Category C teams are high growth teams that thrive off quick wins, highs of achievement, and highs of praise. However, these teams often have interpersonal conflict, animosity, and lack of alignment, which are not sustainable for growth. There is a lot of achievement and quick-win growth but no commonly shared system of behavioral conduct that enables collaboration and progress. Category C teams build their skyscraper on a foundation of sand.

Of course, if you hang out in Category B or C too long, you will likely end up in Category D, which means the environment is not peaceful and there is no progress. Teams in Category D are likely to suffer high rates of expensive turnover, become unprofitable, and eventually die out.

Where is your team?

Maybe it changes day to day. Don't worry if the answer is not Category A - that's why I wrote this book! I have worked with many teams not in Category A and rode the wave as it changed for better or for worse. As a leader, I figured out how, with the help from this ethical system, to reach Category A. Teams that study, understand, and implement this system of ethics in their day-to-day work will reach Category A. This is the place from which you grow sustainably.

Let's study and practice how to reach and remain in Category A.

When the leader sets the tone for peace and progress through action, the team follows suit. However, peace and progress cannot just be preached by the leader to take effect. Peace and progress must be cultivated through a specific leadership mindset, behaviors, and actions. Action toward peace and progress comes from studying, understanding, and implementing the ten ethical principles I present in the guidebook. Throughout the guidebook, we will practice how to move toward Category A regardless of where you feel you stand now. If you feel you're in Category A already, the system will provide additional actions for how to remain in Category A. Leadership ethics is a universal, shared set of guidelines for behavior that enable peaceful collaboration and sustainable progress. The Awake Ethics system sets a new standard for ethical behavior beyond civility and basic moral conduct. As leaders of our work and our life we also must progress and help others on our team to progress as well. Progress is not sustainable without a foundation of peace amongst the team.

The 10 Principles

The Awake Ethics system is composed of ten principles that help leaders cultivate both peace and progress. The ten principles give us a common language for ethical behaviors that result in human-centered progress. When there is no common language, behavior gets messy and people get confused and frustrated. There is no clear way to communicate what the root cause of abstract problems or conflicts are. Have you found this to be true? A framework of principles enables alignment, focus, and clear communication. I have found these principles to be universal because, through my range of experience across many types of jobs, I have seen them aid in decision-making and cultivate both peace and progress.

On the following page, you'll find an overview of the ten principles in order. We'll zoom in on each principle in depth throughout the guidebook.

The first four principles are ethical practices for interactions, which enable peaceful and productive collaboration. We begin our journey with the principle of Truthfulness, which probably feels familiar to most of us. Then things start to get a bit new and different as we study principles two through four. Principles five

The Awake Ethics Principles

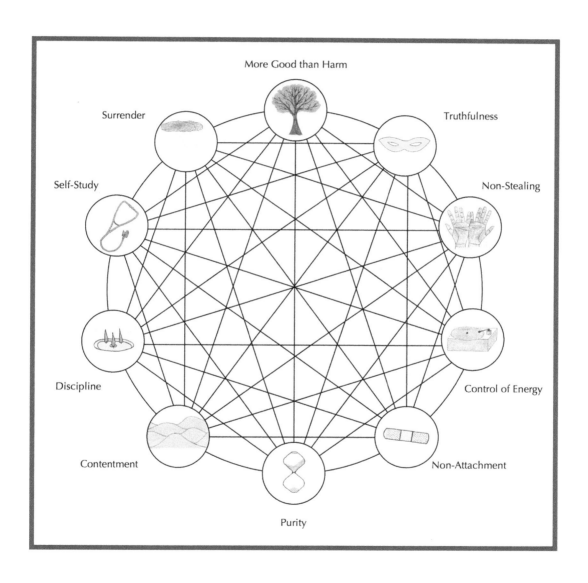

through nine are ethical practices toward ourselves. They are practices of personal conduct that help us reach our highest potential and lead by example. We conclude with the tenth principle: More Good than Harm. This tenth principle is an ethical practice toward ourselves, others, and the world.

Though the principles are presented in a specific order because they logically build on each other and take us through a carefully designed progression, they are all interconnected. Each situation you encounter as a leader may prompt you to use one or more of the principles in conjunction. I suggest working through the sections in the order that I present them but you will find that different sections and exercises speak to your needs and interests at different times during your journey. So, feel free to spend more time and go more in-depth in the areas you prefer. If it sparks your interest and curiosity, it's most likely to stick in your mind and be readily applicable in your work and life. If you identify a need and an application, it's more likely to be manifested in practice.

✎ Working through the Guidebook

Before officially moving on to Part 2: The Ten Principles, let's look at how Part 2 is structured. Each section in Part 2 is dedicated to one of the ten principles. Each section contains an Introduction, Stories from the Field, All in Balance, and Exercises.

✎ Principle Introduction

Each section begins with a brief introduction to the principle. This introduction provides the theory and motivation behind why the principle is important in leadership practice.

✎ Stories from the Field

After the introduction, I present my Stories from the Field. I explain real-life examples that illustrate how the principles have come into play and have helped leaders approach ethical challenges. These stories illustrate common leadership challenges in action to bring the principles to life.

✎ All in Balance

Stories from the Field are followed by a brief All in Balance section. As with any practice, we can overdo it. The All in Balance section explains the implications of overdoing a certain practice and how to stay in check.

✎ The Exercises: Reflection and Actions

Each section contains exercises for putting the principles into action. We often receive a lot of great ideas, advice, and insights but don't quite have the bridge in place to begin using them. The exercises throughout the book are designed to help you start using the principles and integrate them into your leadership of your work and life. The exercises in each section contain two components: a Reflection component and an Actions component.

The Reflections are important because you have to believe in the importance of the principle, by understanding how it plays into your own life before doing the exercises with your team.

As far as the Actions, there are both Individual and Team Exercises. In Awake Ethics, the Individual exercises go a bit deeper. This guidebook is for advanced rising leaders that truly want to deepen their leadership practice in their work and their lives. In many cases, you may read the exercises but decide to skim over them. I would suggest putting aside time to really sit, reflect, and actually write something down. Writing something down is how you start to think in new ways and understand the material. Its like reading an article about how vegetables and green juices are good for you and accepting it as true. However, you go to the grocery store, look at the produce, and then go to the frozen section to buy another case of instant Alfredo pasta and have that for dinner. You can't really know or say that you know the positive effects of vegetables and green juices without experiencing them. You can't know that it is true or that it works without experiencing it. Nothing will change if you don't choose an action and try putting it into real practice. Also, if you attempt to do the exercises with distractions around you, you'll be tempted to skim over them. It takes discipline to take the time to work through them but it is worth it!

✎ The Pace

A book is my favorite way to learn because we can read and work through it on our own time and at our own pace! Books are truly an incredible invention. We don't have to show up at a specific time or place or work at the pace of others. If we want to go back and review or do a section twice or more times, we can. If we want to pause and take a week off, we can. It's freeing and also realistic since we all have different schedules and learning paces. Please see the Author's Notes at the end for a more detailed suggested timeline for working through the guidebook.

Ready? Let's get started!

The 10 Principles

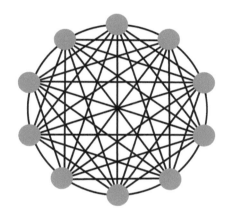

Principle 1

Truthfulness

Truthfulness

Truthfulness serves as the foundation of the Awake Ethics system. Truthfulness is honest, transparent communication. This enables team alignment and authentic collaboration. It seems straightforward that we all should be truthful at work. However, if you pause to think about how often we really feel like we can be truthful at work – to your leader, to your team, to your peers – I'm sure you'll recall a few or many times when it was more comfortable to avoid, distort, or hide the real truth. We don't always feel safe being truthful at work due to the pressure to meet expectations and assume a certain identity. Sometimes it feels safer to keep the mask on. There are often dilemmas about when and how to be truthful, like who needs to know what and why they need to know it. It also often seems as though something doesn't need to be said because it could rock the boat.

Truthfulness is about being honest, transparent, and kind in our relationships with others. Of course there's a balance: in some situations, its better to be kind than right. Truthfulness can be more harmful than productive. We'll talk about this more throughout this section. However, if we're withholding the truth out of fear or rushing through something to get to an answer, it's likely that not speaking the truth is taking away from the team's peace and progress.

As a leader, it's critical to be open and honest and to foster a team culture where transparent communication on your team can flow. This is the foundation of successful collaboration. When we are truthful and receptive, we're able to come into better alignment as a team. Alignment through transparent communication enables us to move as a single force toward our objectives. Truthfulness cultivates trust and progress.

In the Stories from the Field, I present a range of stories to underscore the importance of honesty as a leader. We'll study how to cultivate an environment where your team is confident and truthful. We'll study how to remain truthful and mindful in confidential situations. As you'll see through the examples (and have likely experienced yourself already), truthfulness is challenging in a business environment but it is the first step in moving toward your highest potential with your team.

◆　◆　◆

Stories from the Field

1 Truthfulness with Your Leader

It's difficult to be truthful when we believe we're going to disappoint our leader. Our leader evaluates us largely based on if we are able to meet expectations and follow direction, so it's often scary to be truthful when things are not going quite according to plan.

When talking with my leader, it was always easy to highlight the good aspects of my progress and ignore or glaze over my challenges. One of the instances where it was hard for me to be truthful toward my leader was when he asked the status of a project and I knew that progress wasn't quite where it should be. We were behind schedule because the project testing had not gone according to the plan and multiple partners outside the company, also involved in the project, were not responding timely to requests for inputs. For a few weeks, during meetings with my leader, I reported that everything was fine and it was on schedule. Then I skipped on to change the topic to other things. However, after about three weeks, the project became more and more behind. I realized that I could use some help. I told him that the project was not going quite according to plan and that I needed assistance in getting back on track. When I told him this, I was afraid, but he surprisingly said, "It's okay, we can all learn from the change of plans. Let's work to fix it together." We dug into the details of what the specific obstacles were. He had suggestions for how to engage the project team more frequently and also stepped in, using his seniority, to emphasize the need for attention on the project. There was no time spent on blaming anyone or looks of disappointment. We were able to successfully get the project back on track together.

Let's review. Why was I afraid to tell the truth in the first place? I was afraid to share that I didn't know how to solve a challenge along the way. I was afraid of not meeting expectations and I feared what the consequences may be for my job or my reputation. The fear and uncertainty about the consequences of telling the truth held me back from telling the truth initially. This is very common in leader - team member relationships. I eventually realized that this misalignment between myself and my leader was holding back progress of the team and my own learning, too. I had to gather the courage to tell the truth despite what the consequences would be. I had to trust that by telling the truth with good intentions, the right consequences would follow. Open communication and honesty allowed us to align and join forces in solving the issue so we could move forward. I learned from this experience and I was so grateful that my leader cultivated an environment and relationship where we could be truthful with each other. Fortunately, he took the fear out of the equation so I did not believe that I would disappoint or fail to meet expectations in the future if I needed support. This developed a sense of trust between us and enabled more efficient, seamless progress on the team.

Truthfulness is not just ethical in a sense that it is right. Truthfulness does provide the foundation for collaboration but it also enables progress for all involved. If your leader does not cultivate an environment of truthfulness and remove fear, it may be time to consider sharing that with your leader or seeking a leader that values this principle in practice. Trust is a must. When we're truthful, we can join forces to progress together.

2 Truthfulness with Your Team

As a leader, I found it challenging to be truthful with my team members when I didn't know the answer to something. Other leaders tell me that they have shared the same fear. Saying *I don't know* to your team feels as though you're not meant to be in the leader role - like you're a fake or you are failing to support them. Many leaders hire a brand new team of people so that their personalities mesh but also because the leader wants to know more than the people they manage. It's intimidating to have someone on your team who knows more than you. It can feel discouraging and scary to defer to someone else for the answers.

When I first started leading my team, I taught one member of my team advanced functions in Excel so I could transition a project over to him. I also taught him to use one of the systems we used day-to-day for operational purposes. After a few months, his Excel skills were about the same level as mine and he knew 100 times more about the operational system than I did. I found myself deferring to him to answer complex questions about the system. At first, it felt awkward and as though I could no longer support him if he had a question. Then I realized that I could perform other leadership responsibilities. I had more time and focus. I could let go of the need to know everything. Also, by having him focus and specialize, we actually gained strength as a team. He became the system guru and when we hired new people onto the team, he'd train them on the system efficiently.

Leveraging different skill sets on your team is a part of collaborating and making the whole powerful. I learned through this experience that leaders should be able to identify what skills they don't have that could make the team even better and be honest about it.

Just as you should not fear being truthful with your leader, do not fear being truthful with your team members. You maintain respect by being truthful, not all-powerful. Knowledge is important, however, if you are dishonest, all respect is lost quickly. Acknowledging your own challenges from time to time keeps team members feeling as though they can ask for support without disappointing you or suffering consequences. You must lead by example if you expect them to be confident and truthful in return. They should respect you for your ability to build a strong team and encourage learning and progress.

3 Slowing Down to Find Truth

When presenting in a large meeting or spotlight situation, we often feel pressured and become preoccupied. The pressure of the limelight makes us feel that we need to perform and be the subject matter expert. Even when we fully prepare, unexpected encounters arise that can take us off track. Once, in a meeting with a group of about 40 people, I was presenting a project plan and someone in the meeting asked a question to which I didn't know the answer. I instinctively felt that I should know, as the presenter. Eager to provide an answer, I responded with an answer I thought would suffice: a random number. Then someone else asked, "Well, how do you know that?" Harder. I was left kind of tongue-tied. What was the right answer? The truth was, I didn't know and no quick thinking on the spot was going to get me there right now. I needed to reference and research some things. Why did I just spit out something so random? I then stated that *I needed to look into it* and almost crawled under the table.

Afterwards, I talked with my leader and he told me that it's okay to say *I don't know*. By saying *I don't know, but I'll figure it out*, it is more professional and keeps the meeting moving. Overall, I was prepared for the meeting but just being nervous and eager to provide an answer, I rushed to give an answer before thinking about what she had actually asked and what the best, honest response would be. I realized how uncomfortable I had been in that meeting and that I had made myself look stupider than if I had just said that I didn't know and offered to find out.

Really looking clearly at a question to provide an honest, true answer sometimes takes confidence and patience. It's not only fear of being perceived as unprepared or unworthy that stops us from telling the truth but also just jumping too far too fast to provide an answer. We rush to conclusions to check off the boxes and fulfill requests. It's messy. We could often benefit from taking time to stop, back up, and think before stating an answer. Assuming and answering without thinking causes us to provide misinformation and proceed out of alignment. The fear of immediate consequences often holds us back from larger scale, collective progress. Ultimately, it is not best for the team or anyone involved. It inhibits progress. Sometimes it's worth slowing down to reach the best, truthful solution before proceeding.

4 Feedback

Feedback is a crucial part of participating on a team. Feedback is how we improve individually and collectively. A key leadership skill that is very underrated is how to collect, give, and integrate honest feedback on the team. As a leader, it is important to set up feedback loops on the team and ensure feedback is utilized to enable continuous communication and improvement. Giving constructive feedback can be scary because you don't want to jeopardize a relationship with someone. Constructive feedback can often be taken personally. Managing interests and personalities can be a big challenge. However, giving and receiving honest feedback is part of any collaborative process and critical in continuously strengthening the team as a whole. When working with a team at a retail company, a leader told me that he was struggling to maintain peaceful interactions among his team members. He managed remote store teams as well as teams at the central home office. Weeks ago, he had visited a store to collect feedback from the team there on how the home office team initiatives and communications could be improved over the coming year. The team at the store gave him honest feedback about what they thought was working very well and what they thought could be improved to make workflow more efficient and communications clearer. After gathering the feedback, the leader returned to the home office and shared the summary of feedback with the home office team. Together they planned new initiatives to address the areas for improvement.

Fast forward to a few weeks later when the leader received an e-mail from one of the store team members, Lyle, stating that one of the home office team members, Rachel, had visited the store team that week. During her visit, she voiced to the store team members that she was upset that they had given constructive feedback (or what felt to her like negative feedback) about the home office team's communication and work. Lyle told the leader that this disappointment and animosity from Rachel during her visit made him feel like he could no longer give honest feedback without feeling like it would create animosity.

Rachel had ignored all the positive feedback given by the store team and had taken the constructive feedback personally when it wasn't necessary to feel as though she had been doing her job poorly. The leader was disappointed and asked me what we should do to reconcile this misunderstanding and misinterpretation of feedback.

We concluded that Rachel needed some acknowledgement and to realize all the positive feedback that was given first. She clearly took her work seriously and took pride in the work she did, which is good. However, she needed to realize the value of feedback for her and for the team to continue to learn and grow. She needed to realize that it was not a personal attack on her performance and potential. Over the next week we made sure Rachel was given positive reinforcement for the work she was doing through acknowledgement via e-mail and at meetings. We made sure Lyle knew that Rachel should not have taken the feedback personally, that we would resolve it with her, and that the store team's honest feedback was critical for the progress of the team. The leader discussed with Rachel in a one-on-one touch base that feedback, especially feedback shared in a group setting, is never to be feared or taken personally as though it is directed at one person. It is given in a group so that we can reflect as a team and brainstorm how we can become stronger.

Reframing the feedback in this way gave Rachel positive reinforcement, a sense of trust, and motivation to seek out honest feedback. This mindset shift removed her fear of constructive feedback and turned it into fuel for new potential. Instead of fearing or pushing away constructive feedback, she began to seek it out for her personal growth and for the team.

Honest feedback is how we align and progress. When leaders are closed off and resistant to feedback or listening to the truth, this discourages the flow of feedback. By taking constructive feedback personally and distributing your fear back on the feedback giver, you are stopping yourself from progressing and the team from getting stronger. By shaming others for giving honest, constructive feedback, you create an environment of fear where truthfulness cannot survive and the team cannot progress. No one giving feedback should have the intention of disappointing other team members. If the feedback is given mindfully and honestly, it should be appreciated. If the feedback is not clear, work to understand it. Not all feedback has to be actioned upon but if it is given genuinely, it should be acknowledged without drama and without assuming it is a personal attack.

As a leader, it is important to train and encourage your team to give and receive honest feedback and integrate it into their work to continue to improve. Leader to team member, team member to leader, and peer to peer truthfulness is required to reach your highest potential as a team. We do this by cultivating an environment of compassion and understanding. We do this by showing, through action, that negative consequences and animosity are not the result of telling the truth. The results of truthfulness are peace and progress, through team alignment and collaboration.

All in Balance || Truthfulness

The leader of the team has the responsibility of cultivating an environment where truthfulness is safe and rewarded. However, there are situations where the leader is responsible for keeping information confidential that is personal for team members. The leader is also responsible for cultivating focus on the team by not sharing too much unnecessary content, which we'll talk about more with Principle 3. Sometimes withholding information intentionally is best, especially when it is highly personal information or information that is not relevant for the whole team. There's always a tactful aspect to being a great leader.

When you're on the fence about telling your leader, your team, or your peers anything such as honest feedback, the status of a project, or difficult news, ask yourself: Will telling the truth bring us more into alignment? Will telling the truth to this person help them grow in the long run or is it unnecessary or more harmful to point out something constructive? Am I prohibiting the team from moving forward toward our highest potential by withholding the truth? Sometimes the answer to these questions is No but it's usually Yes: the truth will set you free!

Delivering dishonest information is never the right decision, just like harming anyone is never the right decision. If you're afraid to tell the truth because of fear about the outcome or consequences, then the truth probably does need to be revealed and it will be eventually, in some form or another. You should seek work environments where the truth is supported and encouraged so you can provide the same environment for your team and maximize your potential. Balance kindness and appropriate disclosure with alignment for progress in reaching your highest potential.

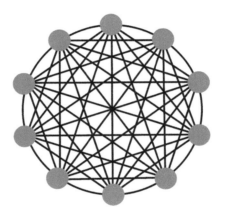

Does your leader cultivate a team culture where truthfulness is encouraged?

_____

_____

_____

_____

How does truthfulness and transparency enable your team to align and progress? How does a lack of truthfulness stop you from progressing?

_____

_____

_____

_____

How do you cultivate an environment of truthfulness for your team members? Have you encountered any challenges in maintaining an environment of open communication and honesty?

_____

_____

_____

_____

Action

Exercise 1: Team Field Notes

Why? Inquiry based on experience is how we learn from each other and build strength in knowledge.

Team meetings are a platform where team members should be encouraged to share challenges and questions, as well as seek support, feedback, and guidance from the team. Field Notes allow the team to share learnings with each other and build collective knowledge. As the leader, you will also become more aware of your team's understanding of their work and where you could help resolve blind spots.

Step 1: Prepare

Purchase field notes journals for your team members. As an alternative, you can of course start by using a piece of paper or a digital journal. However, I think it helps to have a cohesive place to keep this work over time to look back on it week-to-week.

Step 2: Kick-off Prompt

At team meeting, kick off the exercise by asking your team members to keep a list of at least one question they have about their work, the team, or the organization.

Step 3: Share

In weekly team meetings, ask each person to share with the team. When you review the questions the day before, you could prompt certain questions you found interesting and relevant for the team to discuss as a whole. Depending on the size of your team, do this weekly or monthly and allocate at least 30 minutes for the team sharing and discussion. Also ask that they submit the questions to you via e-mail the day before the following team meeting discussion.

Exercise 1: Team Field Notes

Fields Notes Example

Rebecca - Customer Analyst

Weekly Field Notes

Questions!

What is the difference between the sandbox database and the actual database?

Why do we have sub categories for the Tops product category but not for Pants? It seems that there is a lot of variability in the product offering and seasonality and we could benefit from further categorizing Pants for analysis.

How often is inventory availability on the website refreshed? How often does an inventory synch between the system and wbesite happen?

Things to discuss with the team for ideas:

Tech team reported issues with capturing customer zipcodes over the past two months, which effected our customer location analysis and we need to find a workaround solution.

Database additions and upgrades were completed faster than usual this week ahead of schedule, allowing us to complete the monthly reporting ahead of schedule.

When we inquire, we learn and evolve. Encourage your team to be consistently inquisitive about their work and the organization. Build a culture where sharing challenges and progress is encouraged.

Action

Exercise 2: Touch Base Conversations

Why? One-on-one communication is key for building deep trust and for sustainable collective progress.

One-on-one touch bases, between you and each team member individually, are an opportunity to get to know your team members and create a relationship where they feel comfortable coming to you for advice and support. A relationship of trust and truthfulness with your team members is crucial for staying aligned, maintaining genuine respect, and reaching objectives.

Here are tips to keep in mind to build trust with your team members and align.

◆ Always ask about what challenges you can assist with. Don't glaze over issues they bring up or projects that are behind schedule. Stay positive and inquisitive about how you can help them move forward.

◆ Share some of your own relevant, recent work challenges with them once in a while, not as a burden but as a leader leading by example.

◆ Ask them for feedback on your performance. Ask how you could do better or better support them.

◆ A good example of a candid, truthful, productive touch base conversation is given in Stories from the Field I.

Exercise 3: Icebreaker Questions!

Why? Learning about each other while also practicing open communication facilitates open communication and builds trust.

This is a team exercise that helps to cultivate an environment of truthfulness and open communication. Icebreakers do exactly what the name implies: break the ice in communication. They melt or remove communication barriers by getting everyone talking about something they can talk about easily: themselves.

If you begin each team meeting or department meeting with one Icebreaker question, over time people get to know each other better and feel as though they can connect with and be open with their team members. It's important to do it at the beginning of the meeting because it serves as a warm up for open communication during the meeting.

Sometimes it feels weird to start doing team exercises in a business environment if other leaders in your group or organization don't already do this regularly. However, you must lead by example and it is best practice to bring out the human side of your team for authentic, aligned collaboration and progress! You'll be surprised how such simple exercises build connection and enthusiasm.

Turn the page for some of my favorite Icebreakers.

Action

My favorite Icebreaker questions:

If you were limited to following only one person or one influencer, who would you continue to follow and why?

What is the most memorable place in the world you have visited or spent time? Why?

If you could have an all-expenses paid journey for one week to one new place in the world, where would you travel to and why?

What is a company or organization with service or a mission that has really impressed you?

What is a personal or professional obstacle you have overcome? How did it transform your perspective or approach to your work and your life?

What is your favorite childhood book, movie, or TV show?

What is a hobby or tradition you have enjoyed doing consistently throughout your life?

Have you read a book that changed your perspective or approach to life? What was it?

Please also come up with your own!

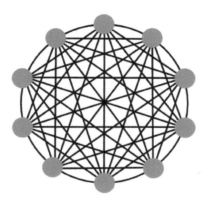

Trust is established through truthfulness over time.

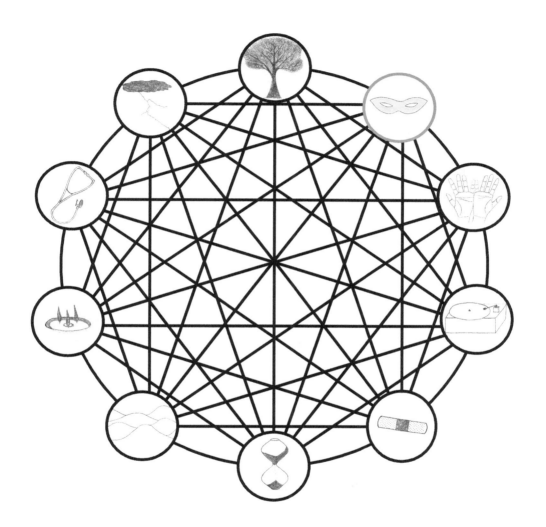

Principle 2

Non-Stealing

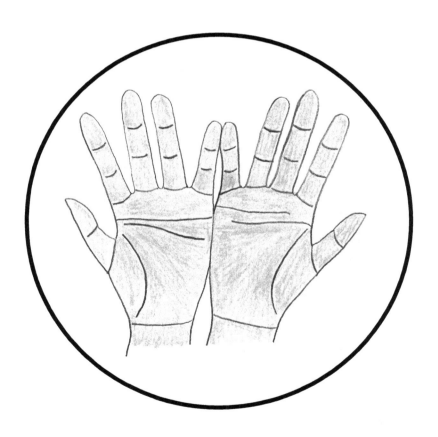

Non-Stealing

While Truthfulness is the foundation for collaboration and progress, Non-Stealing is the catalyst that takes your team's knowledge, skills, and potential to the next level. Non-Stealing does not merely concern stealing material things from our co-workers (though, if that's an issue at your organization you should probably address that). What I'm really getting at in this section is that an important ethical practice for leaders is to not steal experiences and acknowledgement from others. What? I will explain. If we talk about this ethical practice in terms of modern leadership, we can say that it is ethical to give acknowledgement and experiences to our peers and team members.

Do you remember a day early on in your career when you were most excited or felt happiest? Maybe you were given an opportunity to take on a new role or project. Maybe your leader or mentor, gave you an opportunity to contribute something big or learn something new. You felt positive progress, challenge, and possibility. Without the support from leaders within the company or organization, it is impossible for team members to gather experience, build expertise, and develop a point of view.

By giving knowledge, feedback, fair acknowledgement, and relevant experiences to our team members, we lift them up to reach their highest potential. Experience can be in the form of a learning experience, a project opportunity, feedback, or valuable life and career experience. Remember that open hands are not just giving hands; they are also open to receive. By giving these things, we lead by example and show what we would also like to receive. We move toward our highest potential by practicing mentorship and learning from the team members as they progress. When you give selflessly for the good of your team members and their growth, you receive benefits in return. Giving experiences helps each team member develop knowledge, skills, and interests and builds the strength of the team as a whole. As we'll see in the Stories from the Field, there are many ways to offer your team experiences and genuine acknowledgement.

◆ ◆ ◆

Stories from the Field

1 The Gift of Applied Education

When I first started working, I didn't know many practical business tools and concepts. However, I was very fortunate to have an excellent leader. When I joined the team, he spent time teaching me all the tools and information I needed to know. We spent hours discussing the context of the company and how what we did as a team fit into the big picture of the company. Within a year of working with him, I was proficient in Excel and could work on complex data analysis and modeling projects. This knowledge and this way of thinking have stayed with me throughout my career.

My second leader was also a great leader and mentor. Similarly, she spent hours upon hours teaching me SQL for data querying and analytics. Though she was busy and had her own work to do, she saw the benefits of teaching me new skills so she could delegate some of her analytical work to me. She saw that I could learn quickly and instead of hiring someone that already knew SQL, she spent the time teaching me. Not only was I building my skills in SQL but I was also honing my skills in how to learn, which so many of us lose after school.

I didn't realize until later on how lucky I was to have two leaders early on in my career that were such amazing mentors and so giving with their time and knowledge. They could have hired someone that already had the skills and experience but they didn't. Teaching me was actually beneficial for them because they could determine the skills I should develop and how I should learn them. They shaped the way I used the tools and tailored my technique and approach to serve the work we were doing. It was mutually beneficial.

I believe companies and organizations can be the best place to learn because they provide the opportunity to learn and apply your skills in a real-world, live environment. Some professional environments are not a great place to learn on the job but in many industries, learning new skills on the job and having the opportunity to immediately put them to use on real projects are invaluable experiences.

Thinking about this in terms of ethics: how is not giving your team new skills and knowledge considered stealing? As a leader, it is your responsibility to make sure your team is getting the most out of their work experience and continuously learning to improve their contributions to the organization and their individual potential. Just being at work and having a job does not mean someone is learning. The leader must share skills to facilitate development and progress. Educational opportunities are improving in some organizations as companies realize that team members need to know how to learn new things regularly with the pace of change. Learning is a skill in itself. Reaching your highest potential involves learning new things and continuous discovery. Give your knowledge and skills to your team. You'll become a better mentor and teacher. You'll be able to delegate to progress and reach your team's objectives more efficiently.

2 Opportunities Beyond the Office

Another way to strengthen your team is to educate your team about the company context through field experience outside of their normal day-to-day work. I have found that team members often don't know many of the people and partners they work with because teams are so siloed. Also, since many of us now work at desks in front of computers, we lose touch with what we're actually contributing to the world. Understanding the big picture in terms of what goes on outside your immediate team can provide greater understanding and motivation. This results in better quality of work, productivity, and enthusiasm.

One of my favorite experiences as a leader was sending my team to the Port of Oakland. Yes, the Port of Oakland! Why? We were part of the transportation operations team for a large furniture company and most of our products came in from other countries and arrived at the Port of Oakland where they were unloaded and distributed to our stores. In the past, I had been to the Port of New Jersey. On that trip, I remember that so many things came together for me as a transportation analyst. It brought my work to life to actually go there and see live what was behind all the number crunching, versus just hearing about it or seeing photos. So, I wanted to provide this learning experience for my team. I knew this would be a great functional learning and bonding experience. The team learned more about the impact and action behind what we do. They returned more engaged and enthusiastic about our work.

Give your team members experiences that build their knowledge, skills, and experience. By lifting them up, they'll lift you, the team, and the organization.

3 Delegating

One key responsibility that was very difficult for me as a new leader was delegation. I was accustomed to working alone as an analyst. I'd receive projects and tasks from my leader and execute the requests according to my own calendar, which was relatively simple. As a leader, I had the support of a team. It was a new challenge to delegate the work instead of just receiving and executing. What should I delegate and what should I do? What tasks and projects should I delegate to whom?

This is when I learned that frequent one-on-one touch bases and team meetings are critical. During one-on-one meetings with team members, I learned about each team member's knowledge, skills, and interests. During team meetings, the team members learned about each other's knowledge, skills, and interests through conversation and sharing our work progress and challenges. It takes time to really understand each team member's capabilities and strengths but that is why it is important to spend time with them on a regular basis. Once I felt that I could delegate according to each team member's knowledge, skills, interests and volume of work they could manage, I felt confident.

However, I also felt bad asking them to do things "for me". I would always ask, "Is that okay?" after giving them a new task or project. I quickly learned that they actually wanted more new work and wanted to learn as much as possible (as long as the volume of work was manageable so they could remain challenged but successful). I was lucky in that I had an enthusiastic team that welcomed learning opportunities. I realized that I would be depriving the team of experiences by keeping tasks and projects to myself. I began to delegate even the cool projects I would have liked to do and assumed the role of the reviewer and supporter. I learned that leadership is serving as a platform for development and progress.

I have often seen teams discouraged and frustrated with leaders that dump excessive amounts of work on them. I have also seen leaders take the stance that they like being a leader because they want a team to do all the work for them. This is not giving experiences. Giving experiences comes along with mentoring and mindfulness. With great power comes great responsibility. A leader with the power to delegate and give experiences must do so elegantly and in the interest of the team and the organization.

4 Giving Hard Experiences

Not all team members readily appreciate learning and development experiences. Especially when you begin to delegate, you'll likely find that some team members do not want to learn or they do not want to take on additional work. They resist. It's hard to motivate them. However, learning experiences are extremely valuable and necessary for progress. Part of a leader's role is to determine when someone is ready to progress, needs to progress, and needs motivation. If a team member is very resistant, it's worth having a conversation with them about why they're resistant to learning new things or taking on something additional. They may have a valid reason you hadn't realized before.

Also, some leaders don't give experiences or delegate new work to their team because they want to protect their team and make them comfortable. Leaders don't want team members to feel as though they have failed in trying something new. Leaders don't want to see team members frustrated or discouraged. However, this approach causes team members to stagnate. The leader is there to provide development opportunities and to be supportive along the way. If you find yourself in this position, challenge your team members and remind them that taking a risk to learn something new won't reflect poorly on their performance if they work intentionally and diligently to progress.

What about when a team member makes a mistake? If a team member does something wrong, it's also part of their experience to fully understand it. Driven people are overly hard on themselves when they realize they have made a mistake. They quickly learn from the experience but sometimes need support and encouragement to continue. Mistakes are common whenever we try new things. Mistakes will happen. They are part of the learning process. On the other hand, some team members do not take ownership of mistakes; they allow the leader to cover up for them or they cover up or ignore mistakes and keep going through the motions without correcting their action. You should always address a mistake one-on-one with team members if they don't realize or address it themselves. Acknowledge that it happened; otherwise, it may get overlooked and it will just happen again. It is an experience for that person to understand the mistake and learn from it. Learning to understand what went wrong and getting back up is how we grow stronger. Allow team members to experience failure and tough feedback. A leader must serve as a mirror as well as a platform for development and progress.

◆ ◆ ◆

All in Balance || Non-Stealing

Non-stealing is about building strength and providing motivation. Leaders do this by giving knowledge, skills, and opportunities to team members. Can leaders give too much?

When we begin to overeducate team members and don't allow the tools and new skills to sink in, the new experiences are lost. Team members need time to put new knowledge to use. There must be an integration period where team members actually apply the knowledge and skills. In school, people are constantly educated through new rounds of courses but there's rarely opportunity or time for application. Formal education is so focused on intellectual learning and confirmation of understanding only through written tests on the material, not functional usage. The problem with this approach is that the concepts don't really sink in and people don't understand the real-world applications and potential for how to use it beyond the classroom. Concepts learned only intellectually are registered at the surface level of the mind but not at the experiential level. Learning for intellectual entertainment is nice and may be a bonding activity, which is also functional, but learning is much more impactful if team members can use the skills right away. Make sure team members are taking time between learning experiences to apply what they learn to the work they're doing and to understand the impacts. Make sure progress and productivity continue to improve as they collect new skills. Team members will find satisfaction in seeing what they learned put to use. This will move the team members individually and collectively toward their highest potential.

Finally, rest is important. Though rising leaders are eager to learn and work, we can often overdo the learning and working. Many rising leaders, including myself, work on the edge of healthy challenge and burnout. Don't overburden your team with so much education. Really choose the educational opportunities and new work experiences selectively. Allow team members to rest so they have adequate energy to progress and sustain. Make sure to observe and gather feedback from them, since different people learn and integrate information at different paces.

Reflection

Does your leader provide learning and development opportunities for you? What new knowledge, skills, or experience could add value to your work?

_____

_____

_____

_____

How do you provide learning opportunities for yourself? What was the last learning experience you had? If you were to sign up for any course to go deeper into your own career area of interest, what course would you sign up for?

_____

_____

_____

_____

What learning and development opportunities do you provide for your team? What new learning opportunities would be most valuable?

_____

_____

_____

_____

Action

Exercise 1: One-on-One Mentoring

Why? Spending one-on-one time with team members gives you insight into their strengths, challenges, and true interests. They benefit most from your one-pointed focus and attention.

Team members learn on the job but they can also learn the most from you, as we saw in Story from the Field 1. This is important because, as the leader, you learn how well they understand the work they do, where they need gaps filled in their skill sets, and their interests. It is easy to put off spending the time to educate your team because there is always so much work to do.

This month, plan at least one one-hour meeting with each of your team members to review a project or talk about learning and development plans and opportunities.

Through using the prompts on the following page, you will learn more about your team members. You'll help them to think strategically and encourage them to reflect on their work and think about how they're progressing. Leaders that take the time to provide education and integration have the most successful teams. Add your own relevant prompts as well.

Exercise 1: One-on-One Mentoring

Here are three prompts for mentoring meetings with your team members:

1. Project reviews

   ◆ What do you enjoy about working on this project?

   ◆ What do you think could be improved or what are learnings you'll take forward?

   ◆ What are extensions or next steps for this project?

2. Building new skills

   ◆ What new skills or areas of the team (or business) would you like to learn about?

3. Problem solving

   ◆ What's a challenging, time consuming process you do right now?

   ◆ How do you think we could reduce the time or effort it takes without reducing the quality of the result?

   ◆ Should we research new tools that could make it easier or more efficient? Is that something you'd be interested in doing?

Action

Exercise 2: Team Shadowing

Why? Giving team members context and understanding of what other team members do provides valuable learning experience. It cultivates connection between team members, empathy, and synchronicity.

It's important to give team members a chance to learn from each other. Are team members aware of what others on the team do? It's important that team members understand the big picture and how things relate on the team. This exercise also serves as a team bonding experience for team members to share the work they do with others on the team, learn more about each other, and even share ideas for how to improve their work. It gives team members a change from their day-to-day routine and a chance to learn something new outside their usual known realm of work.

Step 1: Facilitate Shadows

Schedule shadowing opportunities that last 1 hour to 1 day for team members to learn about other team members' work and interests. Set a specific objective for the hour-long or day-long shadow. Meet with the team members prior to share the objective of the shadow.

Step 2: Shadow Follow-up

After the shadow, have a debrief conversation with each person separately to gain insights about what was accomplished and learned through the shadowing experience.

Exercise 3: Opportunities Beyond the Office

Why? Team members need to gather insights and inspiration from outside to add to their tool belt and realm of understanding.

1. Context visits: Get out in the field!

Context visits are visits to other parts of your organization, usually relevant to the work that you do as a team. I call them Context Visits because they give the team a broader context for their work. We can often become narrowly focused in on our work, which is good for efficiency, but can inhibit creativity and we can get stuck in our ways. Visits to other parts of the company provide opportunities for team members to learn about the company and return to the office with fresh perspective and ideas. They will also connect with others in the company and form new bonds.

2. Conferences: Network!

Conferences are also a great opportunity for team members to learn. Some conferences are more focused on sales, so research the conference and make sure there are relevant sessions and the other people that attend seem like a good community for networking. Networking broadens the perspectives of team members and also generates new ideas. Conferences are also where team members learn about new tools and the latest capabilities to consider adding to the team.

3. Training Courses and Workshops: Gain specific, relevant new skills!

Finally, training courses are a great opportunity to provide deeper education for your team members. I am a believer in learning through experience but once in a while, going out to purely learn a specific new skill can be very valuable. A lot can often be learned on the job, but encouraging your team members to take in-person or online courses relevant to their field or to learn a new, value-adding tool will add capability to the team and empower them to continuously learn.

Open hands are not just giving hands; they are also open to receive.

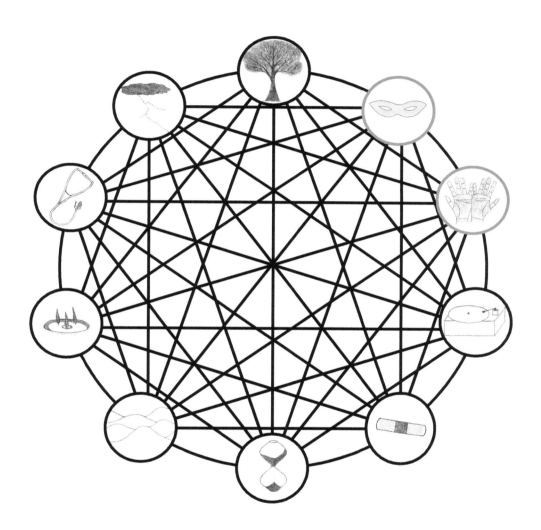

Principle 3

Control of Energy

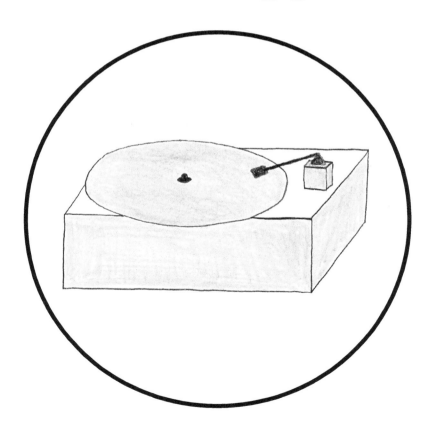

Control of Energy

After establishing a strong foundation for collaboration, it's important to cultivate focus for yourself and your team. Ideas, distractions, and drama arise that we must constantly address and help to reign in the focus of our team members. Control of Energy means using your energy in a way that is most beneficial for yourself, for the team, and for others in order to cultivate focus. It is called energy control and not just behavior control or self control because this practice spans all uses of our energy from attention, to emotions, and actions. As leaders, how we control our own energy and cultivate focus impacts our team's peace and progress.

As an initial example, think about what company politics and drama do: take focus away from the work and create separation between people. This is detrimental to collaboration. Think about what happens when we show up late for a meeting: we feel flustered and don't participate to our full potential. Intentionally channeling your energy toward action that is positive and productive is of utmost importance for leaders to practice.

I know it's harder than it sounds. Physical, mental, and emotional control is a sign of an advanced, Awake leader. How you respond to dramatic triggers and carrots that don't really serve you or the mission of the team says a lot about your strength and ability to focus and progress. By making sure you spend your energy optimally toward your objectives and potential, you won't get caught up in drama and get off track. You can always choose where to place your focus and energy. Just like a needle on a record, if you want to change the song, you can move the needle. It sometimes takes courage and persistence, but you can always choose where to place your attention.

◆ ◆ ◆

Stories from the Field

1 Verbal Delivery

As a project manager on a logistics team, I traveled a lot. Whenever a new team member joined the company, the leadership team would plan a visit to our distribution center and offsite locations to make sure he or she understood the network and met our partners. One winter, a new senior leader named Leah joined the company, so I traveled across the country with a few peers to show her the furniture warehouse. During the tour of the warehouse, Leah revealed another side to her calm, composed demeanor. As we toured the warehouse, she started asserting loudly that the lights were hung too low and that the trash bags were the incorrect type of bag for a warehouse. The team was surprised and uncomfortable with her tone but acknowledged that we'd note all of her suggestions and concerns to address them. She continued to have meltdowns throughout the day and loudly, over-dramatically expressed her concerns. It quickly turned into actual shouting at the warehouse manager and members of our team.

Even after the visit, back at the home office, her negative tone and outbursts continued. We understood that her concerns were valid and acknowledged them; however, she continued to speak with harsh tones and condescending words. Her team members and her peers (myself included), started to avoid her. Some team members would work from home out of fear. Finally, her negative tone and consistent meltdowns caused one of her key team members to resign. This was detrimental to the team's morale and negatively impacted productivity.

When trying to make a point or be heard, think about how you can make the impact and impression you want without negatively impacting others. Could Leah have made her point in a calm, composed manner that people would hear and respect? What type of delivery do you respond to?

It is important to remain mindful of how you deliver verbal communications and control your emotions. We all can learn to control our response to frustrating or unexpected triggers. This is Control of Energy in practice. As a leader, no matter how frustrated you get, there is always a way to convey your point that does not involve raising your voice. It is never constructive to raise your voice, lead with anger, or condition team members to respond to or behave in this way.

Over time, stressful interactions negatively impact the team and become obstacles to our highest potential. Stress also causes long-term damage to relationships and health, which is not a peaceful, sustainable work environment for anyone. A great way to voice concern about someone else's behavior and protect your own energy is to talk with your leader and gain his or her partnership and advice. Schedule a dedicated meeting about it (even if it's short) in order to underscore the importance of the situation and fully resolve it for yourself and for the team.

2 Written Communications

E-mail, instant messages, and phone calls are so prevalent as communication methods in our modern work environments. Everyone has different techniques and tones when writing e-mails. It's important that we intentionally control our delivery of written communications as well, to cultivate focus and positivity. This example is a more serious case of controlling digital delivery.

It was just a few weeks after the New Year. I was excited to hit the ground running with my team and work toward our vision for the year. We had many exciting projects to work on. I came into work on Monday morning and found an e-mail from the CEO in my inbox that had been sent out to the whole home office campus. The e-mail was written entirely in capital letters, detailing how we had recently taken a devastating loss because important product arrived late from our overseas vendors. The vendor made a production error and had to remake a lot of the product for an important, high value furniture collection.

Customers had preordered the product and many cancelled their orders when they were notified that the product would arrive weeks late. The company lost tens of millions of dollars in sales because of these cancellations. To describe his concern, the CEO said that we had basically killed hundreds of customers by allowing this to happen and we needed to URGENTLY work to get back on track.

I understood his disappointment and frustration, however, a few things came to my mind when I read this. Firstly, how was I to address this at my morning team meeting? Secondly, what am I supposed to do and direct my team to do? If I could help, I would but now my team was startled. I was startled as well. It was frustrating because our team had no relation to the root cause of the issue; however, we felt responsible and concerned. How had reading one crazy e-mail thrown off my entirely positive vibe from the weekend? I collected myself, printed the letter, and we talked about it as a team that morning. We made light of it but also acknowledged that it is important to the company, clearly, so we should take it seriously. I suggested we remain open for new requests to help but also zoom out and remain observers. It clearly still affected their focus that day and for many after that, wondering what the implications would be.

So, why was this not ethical delivery of information? Why was this not the best use of his energy? I understood the CEO wanted everyone to be informed and he felt that he needed to convey the importance of the error. However, the delivery threw everyone off and put everyone on high alert with no clear plan of action. Instead of directing focus toward a clear call to action, he directed focus toward worry and unresolved failure. Though the CEO wanted to convey his frustration and passion, he was not rightly using his energy by using the entire company as a stress outlet. He should have directly communicated his concern and made a plan with the key stakeholders only, before alerting the entire company. In terms of his tone, he was letting his emotions run riot. Many responsible employees that had previously respected the CEO and the organization left the company over the weeks following the incident. The focus and productivity in our office – a department that had no direct relation to or control over the instance – was completely thrown off for months.

Before you use valuable energy to convey a point or release frustration, consider if it is the best use, the right audience, and how the message and tone will affect others. When we lead by example and keep the focus and peace of others in mind, we lay the foundation for productivity. When you disrupt the peace, make sure it's minimal and there is a clear call to action. Use clear, focused, positive language whenever possible for the best short-term and long-term impacts.

3 Respect for Time

Time is a container for however we choose to use our energy. Our time is so precious. How we spend our own time is important but in collaborative environments, we all must respect each other's time. Respecting the time of others is respect of energy.

I learned a lot from a leader who provided an excellent example for how to prepare for and execute efficient meetings that kept the team focused and engaged. At many work meetings, I often felt distracted when the agenda or purpose wasn't clear. I felt like some meetings were a waste of time. However, I always felt peaceful, challenged and focused in meetings held by this specific leader. He would always send out a meeting agenda to the participants at least 24 hours prior. While other managers would show up huffing and puffing and a bit late to their own meetings to make sure everyone knew how busy they were, this leader always arrived early and with a calm, collected demeanor. He thought through the purpose and complete agenda for the meeting. Since he was prepared and well versed on his meeting objectives and purpose, he could lead according to the agenda and thoughtfully respond to questions from the team. He never discouraged questions or feedback unless he had already said it earlier in the meeting or someone had already asked it. He kept the team engaged and stayed on track, watching the time and providing only information that was relevant to the discussion. People left with clear action items, feeling energetic and inspired to get to work.

All in Balance || Control of Energy

The result of optimal energy control is peace, focus, and progress toward objectives. When we don't practice energy control, we feel unfocused and our team does as well. However, our energy control can get off balance when we are too strict or reserved with how we use our energy.

Though we should only give information that is relevant, in order to keep the team focused, we also need to remain human. There's a human aspect to leadership. We sometimes need to go off on a tangent in a touch base and talk about our family. We need to spend an extra hour at a team lunch sharing life news. Though this is the exception to everyday best practices, it is important to keep a balance of focus and enthusiasm on your team. The balance between productivity and positive collaboration is so critical in the big picture. It's about the culture that you want to create.

Many leaders tend to lean toward one side or the other: they are either too strict and work-oriented or they always go on tangents, are late to meetings, or constantly get caught up in drama and politics. Which side do you fall on? Can you focus on balancing deep focus with human-centered interactions? If you feel you are too work-oriented, maybe try getting coffee with team members occasionally or planning team events. If you feel you're the type that gets off track, is late, or gets distracted by drama, try making some goals to set parameters and set calendar notifications to stay on track. We'll work on this in the exercises.

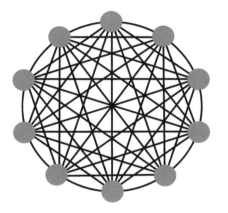

Have you encountered dramatic or political issues in your workplace? What is a specific instance, person, or theme?

_____

_____

_____

_____

What do you do to maintain composure when dramatic or political conversations or situations arise?

_____

_____

_____

_____

What tone of communications do you find most conducive to focus and harmony on your team?

_____

_____

_____

_____

Action

Exercise 1: Bookend Meetings

Why? Cultivate focus, align the team around key objectives, and spark enthusiasm.

If you think about each week as a phase of progress, Monday sets the stage for the work that will be accomplished that week and Friday is the bookend that summarizes and sets the stage for the following week. Use this simple weekly practice to focus your attention on the right areas and align your team around the focus areas collectively.

Monday Meetings

When team members return from the weekend, it's important to reset as a team. Everyone should be focused on the overall team objectives and clear on what their individual objectives are for the week. Ease everyone into the week and outline the week at a collective and individual level, pointing out key milestones to be achieved.

Friday Meetings

At the end of the week, it should be all about acknowledging wins from the week, assessing what objectives for the week were not met, and giving a preview for the next week.

In Friday meeting, return to your Monday meeting objectives. Review them with the team. Highlight or star key milestones that were accomplished and acknowledge the team members. Summarize the team's collective accomplishments and summarize what needs to be revisited or completed next week. It's helpful to leave those items on the white board to remind you on Monday morning about what should be added to the following week's list.

Exercise 2: Team Newsletter

Why? E-align your team's focus around the key objectives, so attention doesn't stray and move toward unnecessary tasks or politics.

Though it is ideal to be able to meet as a team in person, many teams work remotely and frequent in-person meetings aren't possible. It's still important for the leader to be able to align the team around key objectives and cultivate clear focus so the team is able to prioritize and stay motivated.

If you know that in-person team meetings are not realistic on an ongoing basis, create a weekly or bi-weekly e-mail newsletter to send out to your team members. Make the e-mail a consistent format and structure so that the team get accustomed to receiving and reviewing the e-mail regularly.

Monday E-mail Components

Include focus points for the week, key objectives to accomplish by the end of the week, announcements about new team members, and company performance metrics and news.

Friday E-mail Components

Friday wins for the week! Acknowledge team members that completed their week's objectives and any major team milestones completed. Also note key objectives or tasks that were not accomplished or you are behind on, clear delegation as to whom is responsible, and a plan of action to discuss and resolve. You can ask your team members to send you updates on Thursday to include in your e-mail so that it is relevant and comprehensive. Get creative and make a team logo or fun e-mail template to use for sending these e-mails so people look forward to them.

Action

Exercise 3: Positive Written Communications

Why? Make sure your communications have a positive tone and are intentionally written to trigger impactful actions and a positive mindset.

As we saw in Stories from the Field II, written communications from leadership can serve as a distraction or as a focus enhancer. Every communication from leadership is taken seriously and drives either motivation or discouragement.

See the following page for a list of essential written communication check points.

Exercise 3: Positive Written Communications

Written Communication Check Points

◆ *What's the core purpose of sending the e-mail?* Think about the purpose of your communication before you deliver it? What are you trying to achieve? You can always open your e-mail with, "I'm writing to... " to state the purpose of your communication.

◆ *Do you need to send it?* Reread it and decide if it really needs to be sent. Everyone receives so many communications in a day and it can be distracting. Whether it's to make someone aware of a project specification change or to provide a mid-day laugh for your team, think about why you're sending it.

◆ *Is the timing appropriate?* Sometimes communications are too frequent and the team would benefit from less frequent, more informational communications. This allows people to maintain focus on their work and have less frequent distraction. Only send project updates or communications to the team as often as necessary. Keep everyone informed but remember that sometimes less is more!

◆ *Is the audience appropriate?* Reread it and decide if you're adding too many people or missing people from the audience. Make sure you haven't mistakenly added anyone to the e-mail.

◆ *Is your tone positive?* Even if the communication is constructive or urgent, write with a tone that will be digestible for people. Make it easy to read, understand, and take action.

◆ *Is it efficient?* Following the tone, check that you aren't providing too much or too little information. I always leaned toward too much content in e-mails and I spent too much of my own time and others' time on the e-mail. Sometimes a call or stopping by in person is more efficient than writing out an e-mail.

You can always choose where to place your focus and how to use your energy.

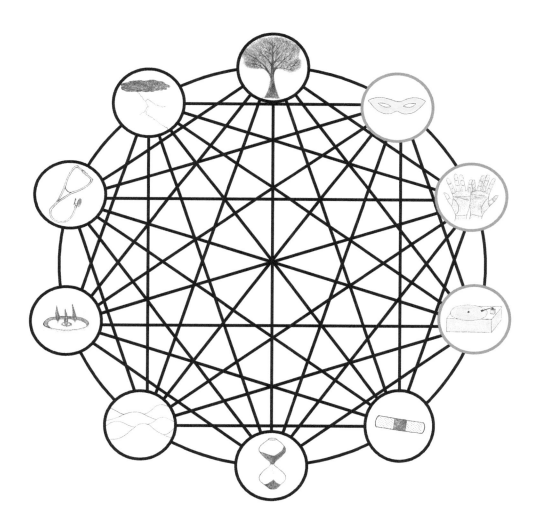

Principle 4

Non-Attachment

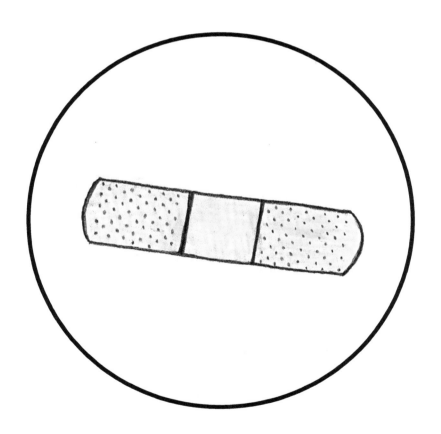

Non-Attachment

So far, we have established that it is important for leaders to foster a culture of alignment and trust, give experiences, and cultivate focus on the team for peaceful collaboration and progress. Non-Attachment, the fourth principle, is the final principle for interactions. Non-Attachment is a challenging principle because it involves letting go of ways and beliefs that no longer serve us. It involves accepting and embracing change. As driven leaders, we have tried and true ways of thinking and doing things. We have set perceptions of what is the right way to execute our work. However, attachment to our ways, beliefs, expectations, and preferences can hold us back. Resistance to change and new ideas often gets in the way of collaboration and progress.

It can feel painful to question our ways and perceptions, like ripping off a really sticky Band-aid. However, Non-Attachment is an important ethical principle to practice as a leader because it enables progress. Clinging to old ways and objectives that are outdated or obsolete gets in the way of welcoming new, more optimal ways of thinking and working. We practice Non-Attachment by reevaluating and letting go of conditioned ways of doing things, beliefs about people, and expectations that no longer serve us and our team. We are then able to welcome new possibility and make progress.

Team objectives, expectations, and standard ways of doing things are indeed important for teams to remain aligned and efficient. However, strong attachment to these systems and beliefs, without consistent reevaluation, causes us to become stagnant. In the Stories from the Field, I will talk about four types of attachment that can be obstacles for leaders: attachment to our ways, attachment to results and gratification, attachment to identity, and attachment to people.

Stories from the Field

1 Attachment to Our Ways

The first and most common form of attachment is attachment to our ways and beliefs. As leaders, we often develop strong attachment to processes and approaches that make us feel comfortable and confident. When we build a tried and true process that works, we can rely on it. However, attachment to certain processes, tools, or the way things are can inhibit progress when better ways of achieving objectives become available.

I once had a leader that had built all of the team data and reporting in an old database system. Though the system was the best option 5 years ago, now there were many more efficient options to run our reporting in less time and with greater accuracy. When I joined the team, one of my first recommendations to him was that we rebuild and transition the databases into a new, more efficient tool. The new system would save us hours of work each week, correct errors, give us the ability to scale, and would be much more user friendly for the team.

At first, my leader was resistant to changing tools for some valid reasons, like the risk of losing or duplicating data. However, I could tell that he was most resistant to learning the new tool himself and changing the current processes, since he knew how to use the old system and could rely on it. He was proud of what he had built and somewhat attached to the tried and true process in place. There is always some risk in intentionally changing something that works; however, the benefits can be immense. After making the case and gaining support from the team to advocate for the new transition, he finally agreed that I could lead the project to transfer all of the data and processes over and rebuild.

Why does this attachment happen to leaders? We have aversion to changing our ways because of risk and pride. It's nice to feel like we have something under control! However, this is never really the case. Change is constant and so it is crucial that we do not get attached to a tool, system, or process. Don't make a specific tool your baby because in a year or two it will probably be obsolete and there will be something more efficient. Learn to accept and enjoy change as part of the natural flow of work and as a challenge to remain innovative and curious. We must not only accept changes that arise but actually lead the change. When we constantly question the way we are doing things and seek out better ways to learn and evolve, we open to new possibility. This practice will lead your team toward new potential and enhanced progress.

2 Attachment to Results and Gratification

The second type of attachment is attachment to results, approval, and praise. Achievement gives us internal satisfaction and gratification through acknowledgement and praise that we receive from our leader, our peers, and our families. We're incentivized at work to achieve and meet objectives, so it makes sense that objectives and expectations are key drivers of our motivation.

Once we start achieving objectives and experience the gratification, we start to become attached to the constant search and capture of achievement and praise. We continue to seek out bigger mountains to conquer and milestones to share with our network and to add to our resume. Have you found yourself running on the endless achievement track? I know the hustle for achievement well. Achievement is not a bad thing but attachment to achieving and meeting idealistic results and expectations can burn us out and lead us off track. Pushing others to achieve can often burn bridges and derail sustainable progress.

One of the early career project opportunities I had was to implement a powerful, expensive piece of software. I saw this as the perfect opportunity to learn something new and also accomplish something impressive. To my delight, after a lot of legwork, I got exactly what I wanted: the approval to begin the project. I had a big mountain to climb over the next year to prove the value of this tool. I had an intern helping me for a portion of the project but otherwise I was on my own. A few months later, the project proved to be much harder to execute while also doing my other work. The results of the initial stages of the project were messy and not the high-impact results I'd wanted to present. I was losing motivation and couldn't quite see how to move forward. I'd stay up late at night worried about how I'd achieve what I'd promised to myself and others. I was too proud to ask for help; I had to do it alone. In the face of all this difficulty and stress, a few months later, I abandoned the project all together.

In hindsight, I don't regret what happened. I learned a lot about my attachment to my pride, ideal results, and achievement through this experience. This strong attachment caused me to actually burn out all together instead of thinking creatively and reaching out for help to get back on track. I was attached to an all-or-nothing result. I did not ask for help because I thought that would taint the success factor. When we resist vulnerability and attach to pride, we negatively impact the success of the team and the organization. This practice of Non-Attachment allows us to move toward higher potential. It also relieves stress by taking the focus off us and our individual achievements alone as the ultimate measure of success. Ultimately, what we achieve together is more powerful and more important than our individual achievements alone.

3 Jealousy and Attachment to Status

The third type of attachment is attachment to things and the desire for things that others have. When we work on teams and in office environments, with many other people around us, comparison is inevitable. This is how jealousy arises. We have that relativity of ourselves versus others the whole day. We're taking it in whether we consciously realize it or not. What do they have that I don't? What did they get that I didn't? We're comparing ourselves with others in terms of what we're contributing, behavior, acknowledgement, image, and even age. In business, jealousy often happens when someone gets a promotion that you wanted or a benefit that seems like special treatment.

Once, as a new leader, I requested a private office because I found that it was too noisy in the open office space to focus on my work and take calls. This proved to be a controversial request and decision for the management because there weren't enough offices for all the mid-level leaders. It came down to determining whether I was asking for the office to sincerely be more productive for the organization or just because I wanted it. Was it the best decision to give me the office or to ensure that everyone got equal treatment so that no one would become jealous?

My office was finally was approved and I moved into the office as a shared space with one other team member. I wasn't attached to the idea of having an office but it did help my productivity a lot. Luckily, no other mid-level leaders were jealous or attached to the idea of an office. However, this often isn't the case. So often, when we see someone else with something, we feel like we should also have it or we need it. When you feel jealous, ask yourself if it is because that thing could actually improve your work and conditions or because you feel you should have something just because someone else does. There have been many times when I have caught myself wanting something that someone else has and then I realize that I'm actually better off without that thing. Letting a desire go can actually improve your focus. By removing the distraction of jealousy, you can continue forward on your path.

When we're too focused outward, on our identity versus others, we get caught up in jealously, which causes misery and distraction from our highest potential. I have found that letting go of jealous feelings frees you from the horrible feeling of animosity. This practice is essential for collaboration. Only you know if something will move you and the team toward new potential. If you feel jealous, try letting it go and embracing the resources you already have while also being real about what new possibilities and resources could lead you toward higher potential.

4 Attachment to People

Finally, the fourth attachment that leaders often face is attachment to people. We often find ourselves attached to people we enjoy working with. We all attach to our team members for different reasons and that's okay. We get used to having our team in place and running smoothly. Retention is also a metric for success that we cling to as leaders to assess our performance. For me, personally, I would attach to my team members because I got to know them as people and enjoyed their presence. It's easy to feel as though a person on your team, especially someone you hired, is an asset and no one else could fill their position. It's not only their skills but also their vibe, their enthusiasm, and who they are as a person that makes them an irreplaceable asset.

I worked with a leader once that called me one night so upset that his star analyst had given his notice and had decided to work for another company. The analyst had been on the team just over a year but was a high performer with great energy. I told this leader that I understood and felt his pain; however, think about what new possibility this is offering for your team's potential. Think about what new possibility there is to recruit someone with an even better skill set. Also consider the new possibility for that analyst along his journey. When we reframed it in this way, it was like the dark cloud started to drift away.

People change; they come, they stay, they go. When we detach from expectations and consistency, we eliminate resistance to change, which is a waste of energy. When we reframe change as a positive opportunity, we become excited and motivated, not depressed and negative. Especially in dynamic organizations, where there are so many changes and progressive people, it can feel like a revolving door of constant change for many different reasons. When change happens, practice framing it as an opportunity to reflect on how it will bring you, your team, and all involved further toward your highest potential. The reality is that, as mentors, we should expect and actually hope that our team members eventually move on whether it is moving toward new responsibilities, into another position on the team or in the company, to another company completely, or up into our own position!

Always ask: What is the best that can happen? An Awake leader can see everything coming together when others are programmed to only see everything falling apart. It is often the role of the leader to see clearly and help their team embrace change as progress.

All in Balance || Non-Attachment

Non-attachment to our ways, beliefs, preferences, and people allows us to embrace change and progress. However, we also must set a vision and expectations so that the team is aligned around the goals. As I mentioned in the introduction, having a clear vision and striving for something individually and as a team is important because we need direction in order to work together. As with all of our principles, it takes tact to balance structured direction with staying open to new ideas along the way. By clearly setting expectations, you can align as a team and know where you're going together. This is key for collaboration. Otherwise, people are all working in their own directions and at their own pace. It often causes frustration among team members. However, don't make the vision or result too fixed or timeless. As we have talked about, when you set a strict vision or result in terms of timing or specifications, it often limits new possibility and integration of change. It also causes attachment and disappointment among team members if things don't go as planned. Find the balance between defining objectives and leaving some pieces open to possibility along the way. The ideal vision and result may change along the way and be better than you had originally planned.

Also, before adopting a new process or tool, assess it to see if it's really beneficial. If we're too open to any change that is proposed or comes our way, we lose our point of view and become passive. As my accountant says, sometimes a Post-it note is all you need. We don't need a new fancy tool for everything just because it was invented, right? Question if you're attached to the old and of course, ask: Could keeping an open mind and at least considering something new and different lead us further toward our highest potential as individuals and as a team?

Be real about what desires are weighing you down and what you're attached to as a leader. Are there stale processes or assumptions that seem to be weighing you and your team down? The Reflection questions and Exercises will reinforce the mindset shift to Non-Attachment.

Are there ongoing processes on your team that you have not revisited in a while? Do you feel that you are attached to any process or way of doing things that could be done more optimally or with more ease?

_____

_____

_____

_____

How do you measure your own success? What is your own definition of success for your work? What specific accomplishments make you feel successful?

_____

_____

_____

_____

Are there limiting beliefs that you (or your leader) are attached to, that may be limiting individual or collective potential?

_____

_____

_____

_____

Action

Exercise 1: Team Brainstorm

Why? When you take time to question your current ways of thinking and doing to explore new options, more creative and more efficient solutions often emerge.

A **brainstorm** is a process for coming up with new ideas. We can brainstorm alone or as a team. We use the word **brainstorm** so much in professional settings that most of us have become totally numb to how funny the word brainstorm is. Am I the only one that thinks a brainstorm sounds painful? Brainstorms are actually really great. I lead a lot of brainstorms but the word has always made me laugh. Anyway, in this case, the word brainstorm is actually appropriate because we're going to stir up the way we think about the way we do things on the team.

In this exercise, you'll brainstorm what could be improved and help you evolve as a team. By bringing attention to what you currently do and asking what could be improved, solutions follow. Including all team members is important because each person will bring different perspective and expertise that adds value to the brainstorm.

This exercise is perfect for practicing Non-Attachment because we're creating an open platform for team members to question our current ways and offer up new ideas.

Exercise 1: Team Brainstorm

Supplies

- ◆ Whiteboard or large Post-it board
- ◆ Dry-erase markers or regular markers
- ◆ Scratch paper for each team member to write notes on

Background on the Mind Mapping Technique

Mind Mapping is a technique developed by Tony Buzan. Mind Mapping is an excellent tool for enabling both design and technical thinkers to collaborate. Mind Mapping has many applications but I love to use it for brainstorming because it shows the team's collective thought process. Let's take a look at how to use Mind Mapping for your brainstorm.

Action

Exercise 1: Team Brainstorm

Step 1

Begin with a central topic. For example, your topic for the brainstorm could be Team Improvement Opportunities.

Step 2

Start to branch. To create the first layer of the mind map on Opportunities, make your first layer of branches areas for opportunity that the team comes up with. Is there a lengthy cumbersome process? Is there a task that never gets done on time?

Step 3

Once you have your first layer, then begin to branch off the first layer of bubbles by asking the team to come up with why they suggested the item in layer 1: What are the current issues or gaps?

Step 4

Finally, add a fourth layer with ideas for resolution. What could be done to solve the issues, identify the blind spots, or explore and implement the opportunities for improvement? Spend at least one hour on this exercise. The more time you spend, the more ideas will arise.

Step 5

After creating your map, write down the opportunity ideas for resolution projects. Clearly prioritize the initiatives based on what is most pressing and also what is easiest, low-hanging fruit to tackle. Make sure to clearly delegate who is responsible for which initiatives and the timeline to complete them.

Exercise 1: Team Brainstorm

The map below shows the general format.

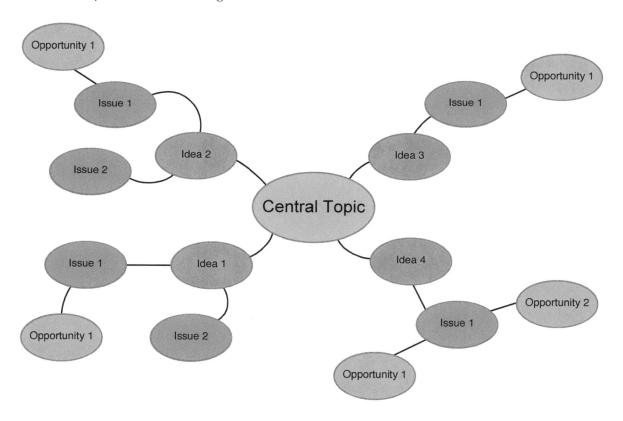

It takes time to hone your skills at artful mind mapping and brainstorming.
Let's take a look at the example on the following page to illustrate the
process in practice.

Action

Exercise 1: Team Brainstorm

An Example in Practice: Improvement Opportunities Brainstorm

The map on the facing page is an example from a small apparel clothing company team.

To follow one arm and their collective thought process, let's walk through the highlighted Inventory Reconciliation opportunity:

Someone from the team mentioned that inventory reconciliation is a pain point or opportunity for the team to improve. They said it was because it's often inaccurate, it's a lengthy and time-consuming process, and they feel there aren't enough people on the team to help achieve it successfully. The team then suggested that they should explore new technology and also spend time over the next month looking at the process as a whole to simplify it.

You can see other similar thought processes reflected in the other branches.

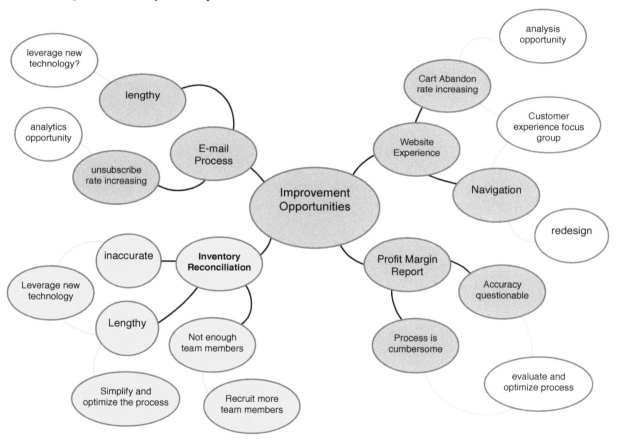

Exercise 1: Team Brainstorm

Example Mind Map for Improvement Brainstorm

When inquiries and opportunities arise, solutions follow! We detach from old ways and start to think in terms of evolution and progress. In the next exercise we'll talk about how to action on your brainstorm ideas.

Action

Exercise 2: Fresh Ideas and New Tools

Why? Gain new knowledge and experience helps us to proactively reflect on our current ways of doing and thinking, and enables us to bring in fresh approaches that help us pivot toward more optimal progress.

As we talked about in Story from the Field 1, Attachment to Our Ways, we must learn to constantly seek out better ways of doing things and not resist change when it leads to enhanced progress.

On the following page are easily accessible ways to discover new opportunities and practice having an open, curious mind. These suggestions can also serve as follow-ups to Exercise 1 for actioning on your brainstorm takeaways by researching and kicking off the improvement initiatives.

Exercise 2: Fresh Ideas and New Tools

At the Office

1. *Share knowledge*: Reach out to peers at work and schedule meetings or coffee chats to discuss ideas. You could even start a monthly innovator's lunch or coffee chat to continuously share ideas among like-minded rising leaders. This includes activities like the Brainstorm from Exercise 1.

2. *Independent Research*: Conduct your own independent research periodically via online publications or trade magazines for the best new tools and practices related to your field and role.

3. *Team Brainstorm*: See Exercise 1.

4. *Strategic Improvement Projects*: Many ideas for improvement often result from brainstorms. Make sure to outline projects with clear timelines and milestones and action on them!

Beyond the Office

1. *Conferences*: Conferences are a great opportunity to network with people in your field and learn about the latest best practices and resources.

2. *Courses*: Whether online or in-person, courses bring together like-minded people interested in learning the same concept or tool. By talking with people in the course, you can learn if they are applying the knowledge in ways that you might not have thought about. Keep in touch with peers to connect about best practices and new resources.

By letting go of our preconditioned ways of thinking and doing that no longer serve us, we are able to welcome new possibility and progress.

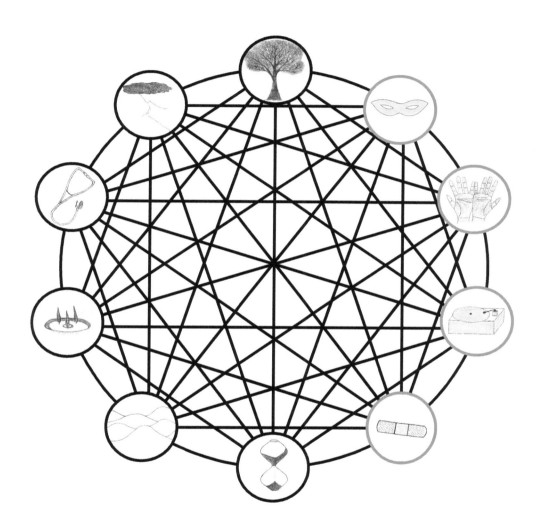

Principle 5

Purity

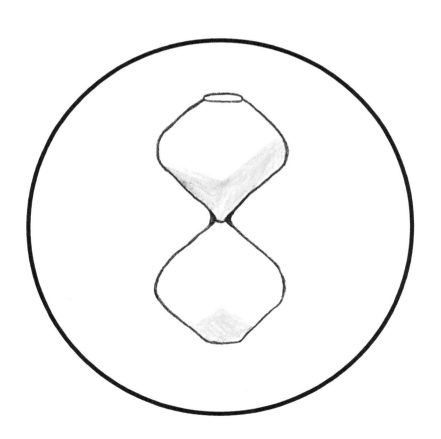

Purity

Purity is the first of the five ethical practices for personal conduct. It is the foundational ethical practice toward ourselves. Have you ever arrived at work feeling overwhelmed or frustrated, and don't quite know where to start? Have you felt burdened by an overwhelming stack of tasks and to-do's and felt like running away from them? Though technology makes our office feel cleaner by eliminating physical paperwork and storage, our computer is often a messy dumpster of digital files and downloads. As we accumulate content, our mental capacity to keep everything organized is strained. Practices for keeping our space, mind, environment, and calendar clean and clear free us from feeling overwhelmed and allow us to move toward our objectives with more ease.

In the ancient system, this ethical practice is about purifying ourselves, our space, and our mind to do our best work and live our best life. It does traditionally include hygienic cleanliness and health practices that make us more able to show up in the world and collaborate. When I speak about Purity as a leadership practice, I'm not talking about a religious kind of purity. Practicing Purity simply means that you maintain a clean workspace, a carefully cultivated work environment, a clear and focused mind, and time management practices (a clean and organized calendar) that allow you to do your best work. The hourglass is always draining. Time is passing by. How do you spend it?

Having routines for keeping our space clean and organized helps us to remain aligned and focused so that we can show up for others and move toward our highest potential. It seems simple but it's a pretty big deal and this practice can make all the difference in whether we achieve our objectives and produce our best work or not. When we show up with a clear mind, we can produce quality work, lead with confidence, and offer support. We can more successfully reach our highest potential with our team. In the Stories from the Field, we'll look at how Purity is an essential part of our leadership practice for finding both peace and more impactful progress day-to-day. We spend quite a bit of time on exercises in this section and that is because the exercises are important for all the other principles that follow. The exercises in this section have been game-changing tools for me in my leadership of my work and life. I'll show you why in my Stories from the Field.

◆ ◆ ◆

Stories from the Field

1 Our Workspace

Doing something as simple as cleaning up your desk or office can do wonders for cultivating better focus. Cleaning and organizing regularly eliminates distractions and makes relevant information and resources easily available. Not only do I need a quiet, familiar environment to do my work but I also need a clean workspace. I have often found myself having a hard time focusing on the task at hand and then I realize – I need to clean! At first, I wondered if this reaction was a way of procrastinating. However, I realized that when my space is organized and clean, I feel as though I have a clean slate to begin my work. I have found that "clean space, clean mind" is true for me. Is it true for you?

It's not just our physical space that can distract us but our digital space as well. It's easy to forget about this. Our computers and phones have become part of our environment, whether we like it or not. We choose it; it doesn't have to be this way. You can ignore the fact that it's messy and unorganized if you want, but notice how that may reflect in how you think, how you feel, or how you produce quality work (or not). Notice how having an organized space can save or cost you time. I am the worst at remembering to clean and organize my computer folders. It's one of those things on which I procrastinate for months until I spend seven hours trying to find an old file and finally say, "Okay! Fine, I'll organize so this never happens again." It promotes ease and efficiency.

So, why is it ethical to keep our physical and digital workspace clean and pure? It's ethical because cleanliness enables us to focus and in turn more efficiently and easily reach our highest potential. Purity is about simplifying. However, Purity doesn't mean that we give up all our possessions and have nothing. Purity means that we're intentional about how we use and maintain our space so we can do our best work, make progress, and show up for our team.

If you think about it, this physical space aspect of Purity is like practicing both Non-Attachment and Control of Energy towards yourself. By first detaching from any unnecessary possessions and clutter, you then eliminate distractions and can focus. You open up space for more time and more clarity about your vision. Starting with your physical space is the key to cultivating deeper focus and removing blockages to clarity and progress. What is serving you and what is distracting? Do you have systems and rituals for cleaning your space? We will try out ways to put this principle into action in the exercises.

2 Our Environment

Beyond our personal workspace, the environment we work in has a huge impact on the quality and quantity of our work as well as our experience. There are so many factors that contribute to a conducive work environment. This aspect of Purity is about continuing to create the conditions for focus and feeling good in your environment. This enables us to do our best work and make sustainable progress.

With more options than ever for where to work and how, it's important to figure out what conditions work best for you. No single environment is ideal for everyone. The optimal environment depends on a lot of factors like personal needs and the type of work you do. I do some of my best writing in coffee shops rather than at home because I love having people around and the sounds and smells of a cafe contribute to my inspiration. However, when I need to do analytics or new creative work for my clients and partners, I need the quiet environment of my home or office.

The most challenging work environment I ever experienced was an open office space. My neighbor had group conference calls constantly, all day at his desk. The office also allowed dogs. Dogs change the environment completely and, depending on the day, it's the best policy or the worst policy ever invented. It was so hard for me to concentrate. It was not sustainable and I sought out a new spot quickly when I realized I was not able to concentrate (and I was going insane!). After that experience, I sought out quiet office environments for my analytical work and phone calls. The biggest failure is when we aren't even aware of what helps versus hurts our productivity and happiness. We don't all have the luxury of choosing our work environment - I have been there and it's frustrating. We can adapt to certain environmental conditions, however, it is often not sustainable and we don't produce our best work. Even small changes help. You may not need to change everything or find another job. It is best to be honest with your leader about what you really need in order to do your best work.

What about your technology environment? I'm not just referring to your technology workspace and how it's organized but how you interact with it. When someone is messaging you on your interoffice messenger, someone is texting you, you're getting e-mail, you're getting phone calls, and you're trying to write a report, how is it even possible to complete any of that report and have it be of quality? Do you set up technology parameters for success?

As leaders, the best we can do is set up our environment in a way that supports our best work and happiness. With experience, we learn what our truly pure work environment is and what doesn't serve us. For our teams, we can point out when we think their environment – how they're leveraging technology or where they're sitting in the office – may be impacting their quality of work. However, only they know if their environment is optimal. It's a lot about feeling and this reflects in our results, too. As leaders, we acknowledge, listen, and respond to their calls for an environment that is conducive to productivity and enthusiasm.

3 Our Mind

Clearing our space and designing our optimal work environment are key for focusing on our best work and progressing toward our objectives. However, no matter how clean our space is and how amazing our environment feels, sometimes we still have thoughts flying through our heads and concentration is difficult. Our lives at work and personally are always changing. Thoughts constantly arise that grab our attention.

What brings on flurries of thoughts? Think about it. When have you felt like your thoughts have been spinning and you can't totally focus? Does it happen when you have an uncomfortable encounter or meeting? When something exciting happens? There are so many triggers around us all the time. Though we can build a barrier to keep the triggers away, we can also practice techniques that help us deal with the thoughts and refocus. For me, flurries of thoughts are usually brought on by new, urgent requests. Change management and prioritization can bring on thought junk, impulsive reactions, and stress. They take me out of the flow of my work. If we don't have methods for responding to thoughts and calming our mind, we quickly burn out because our attention is split in so many directions. Have you ever felt this way?

Also, we can't do our best work when our attention is really somewhere else. Multi-tasking and splitting focus just means we're diluting our focus on each thing. Let's be real. I could always tell when my team members had thought junk going on and were preoccupied. In touch bases, I would explain something and they'd look back at me with a blank stare. I'd say, "Did you get that?" They'd say, "Oh, sorry, I was thinking about something else, can you repeat it?" This happens when we have a lot on our minds, which is most days.

Cultivating practices to clear our minds, prioritize, and continuously return to focus on our work is important. Without one-pointed attention, we cannot work optimally. I have found many techniques work well to clear my mind. I'll share these techniques in the exercises.

4 Our Time

This aspect of purity is possibly the most important to me. I have seen so many leaders struggle with having a clean slate or an organized schedule they actually follow. When someone says they are busy, there are usually opportunities to clean and organize.

One leader I worked with needed help organizing the responsibilities of her team so she could focus more on strategy rather than day-to-day tasks. She said that she's so busy that there is no time to focus on strategy and forward-thinking projects. She said that between managing the team, her personal life, and daily requests, it was just too much. There wasn't a great grasp of really looking at how she was using her time and it made it seem useless to try. She was drifting. The same thing had happened to me as a leader. I would often come into work early in a huff from the commute, I'd run to a meeting, I'd check my e-mail for a while, and then someone would stop by my desk and talk for a while. By the end of the day, I'd feel like I hadn't made much progress. Why did I feel so busy but like nothing was really getting accomplished? I realized that I needed a change of approach. I found that the key was zooming out and making a plan ahead of time to provide direction and structure for my day. So, at the end of each day, I would take a look at my calendar tasks for the next day and actually plan how the next day would be spent. I knew that, given the nature of the work environment and my role, I'd have ad-hoc requests from my leader. However, having an initial ideal plan for how each 30 minutes or 1 hour should be spent would keep me from getting side tracked in conversations or checking my personal e-mail constantly because I had a plan to follow.

When I plan the work and work the plan, I am more productive, have more space in my calendar, and work in flow. I did the same exercise with the leader that reached out to me. It was interesting to see that setting a plan wasn't stressful because we acknowledged beforehand that unexpected things would come up. When working in an organization, you'll always get unplanned requests. Unexpected changes happen. If everything didn't happen and get accomplished exactly to plan, she could incorporate that unfinished work into the next day by taking it one day at a time. Instead of making it stressful by planning out everyday for a whole week and making it seem like a marathon, we planned day-by-day to keep it flexible. We also realized that by having that focus and structure, she had more time! We found two hours per week on Friday afternoons that she could spend with team members brainstorming and strategizing. We'll work on purifying your calendar and an approach to time management in the exercises.

All in Balance || Purity

Can we refine our space, environment, mind, and calendar too much? As a minimalist, focused person I'd love to say No! However, the reality is that, yes, over purifying can take us off balance.

Purity is about focus and happiness. By cleaning our space, cultivating an ideal environment, clearing our mind, and cleaning our calendar, we are making space. We are making space for focus and one-pointed attention. However, purifying is there to support our work, not to be our work. When we begin to use the cleaning practices as means for procrastinating, then it's not fulfilling its function. The cleaning is not our work; it's a foundational practice that supports our work in moving forward toward our highest potential. So, find the cleaning practices that are right for you and then move on in accomplishing your work and progress. Also, do not purify to the point of suffering. What I mean is, you can still have some fun things in your office and engage in conversations for the joy they bring.

Purifying is essential in order to stay focused, organized, and produce our best work. We're conditioned to think more stuff is good: that another frame on our desk will make our day that much better and a side conversation will reenergize us and make us feel more connected. We fall into patterns of how we use our time that begin to feel natural or as though it's a given but really don't contribute to our work or our joy when we overdo it and lose our focus. Only you can design an ideal environment for yourself and only you truly know what fuels your best work. Challenge yourself to think on the simpler, cleaner side of the spectrum than what you assume or you are used to.

How does your current work environment cultivate the conditions for your best work? What aspects don't serve your best work?

_____

_____

_____

_____

What is your strategy for staying focused and maintaining clarity day to day?

_____

_____

_____

_____

Do you feel that you manage your time optimally? Do you have methods for time management that help you achieve your vision efficiently?

_____

_____

_____

_____

Action

Exercise 1: Soji

Why? Rituals help to facilitate a structured way to do a seemingly tedious or mundane task that easily gets put to the side. Cleaning is crucial to maintaining clarity and fueling your best work.

Soji is a Zen practice. It goes something like this: Everyone in the temple participates in cleaning the space for 20 minutes. Each person receives a different assignment and when the bells rings, everyone cleans according to their assignment. After the 20 minutes, the bell rings again and no matter where they are, everyone stops and goes back to their daily rituals.

I love this structure because so often when we set a time to something – when we know it's a 20-minute commitment - our mind focuses and it feels achievable. When we set achievable expectations and make it a ritual that we enjoy, we develop those patterns and practices and it becomes normal and easier.

The Exercise

By yourself or as a team, try Soji as I described it. Find a bell (a real one or a digital one) and set a timer for 20 minutes. Turn off your computer screen and your phone and spend the 20 minutes with the intention of cleaning and organizing your space. See what happens. Hold yourself to doing this once per week for five weeks in a row. You can do the same for organizing your computer files. Instead of turning off the computer screen (of course) just turn off your e-mail and messenger.

Exercise 2: Your Optimal Environment

Why? Environmental factors impact our mindset and the quality of our work more than most people realize. Most leaders don't take enough time to reflect on what's working and what isn't until it's too late.

When you think about your ideal working environment, what does it look like? Often when we can envision it, it can become reality, I have found. What aspects would you maintain from your current environment? What aspects would you eliminate? What aspects would you add? Why?

Draw it out. Think about the intention behind each aspect and item you chose. You can view my example in the Author's Notes.

Action

Exercise 3: The Mind Stuff

Why? When we have a lot going on, we must have practices for allowing the mind chaos to settle, cleaning out the thought junk, and staying the course.

Sometimes concentration is difficult because we have so many thoughts circling. Thought junk can burn us out and make it hard to prioritize and focus. I have found that sometimes doing what may seem counter productive - taking time away from the work - can help to clear my mind and return feeling fresh and focused.

Here are some exercises that help to calm and purify the mind.

◆ Listen to a favorite song or album
◆ Read a book, a passage, or a poem
◆ Take a walk in nature
◆ Talk with a friend
◆ Write
◆ Practice Yoga
◆ Meditate (for at least 20 minutes)
◆ Exercise (solo, non-competitive exercise)
◆ Take a coffee or snack break alone or with a friend
◆ Play a game of Sudoku
◆ Read a chapter of a book
◆ Read a favorite blog

Exercise 3: The Mind Stuff

Once we have calmed our mind and allowed the chaos to settle, we often can return to work rested and rejuvenated. Sometimes we resolve something that seemed very complex when we get space from focusing on it and allowing thoughts about it to take over. We even have a more positive attitude and approach to our work as well.

If you can carve out 20 minutes each day, before and/or during the workday to do one of these exercises that is most beneficial for you, it can cultivate exponentially more focus throughout the day and you will feel as though you have more sustained energy.

Realize that when we calm and purify our mind, our focus and attitude often improve and we can better provide clear direction and focus for our team members. We control our energy more optimally. There are connections between all of the ethical principles but this is a key connection to note. It's a perfect example of how practicing ethics toward ourselves lies the foundation for peaceful, productive collaboration with others.

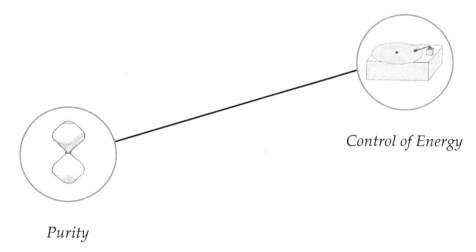

Control of Energy

Purity

Action

Exercise 4: My Process for Time Management Success

Why? Time management and prioritizing is a common obstacle for busy leaders. It's important to have a simple but impactful method for prioritizing.

Those who work with me know that I am very into time management and optimally using my time, whether it is for the creative work or technical work that I do. A plan for how you'll use your time actually opens up freedom to feel as though you know that everything will get accomplished or gives you the ability to proactively reorder and redesign your plans.

Here I will give you my tried and true formula for time management, similar to the solution I described in Story from the Field 4.

Step 1
Start at the week level. List out all of the tasks, projects, calls, and meetings you have coming up that week. List both personal and professional. Just list it all out.

Step 2
Next, take that list you made in Step 1 and assign a day of the week to each task or meeting. For tasks, you may need to start with the day they need to be completed and work backwards to then assign the days you'll work on them.

Step 3
Plan by day. On a new sheet of paper, begin with Monday. List all the tasks you had assigned to Monday on your first list from Step 1 & 2. Do the same for each day of the week so you have a list of tasks for each day.

Exercise 4: My Process for Time Management Success

Step 4
Assign time allowances and/or actual time commitment for each task or meeting. For example, assign two hours for writing up a project scope document or one hour for running errands. If you have a meeting from 3-4pm, note that time commitment next to the task.

Step 5
Finally, on a third sheet of paper, begin with Monday and rewrite the tasks for that day in chronological order (planning your day's schedule) and assign the approximate time you will do each one.

Step 6
Reorganize as needed if you find that there are too many tasks on a given day or scheduling conflicts.

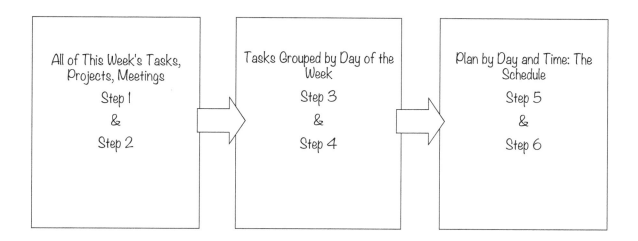

Action

Exercise 4: My Process for Time Management Success

Some Notes

I don't want to get too detailed here with examples and direction. Try out my simple directions and adapt them in a way that works for you. I like doing this by hand on a notepad each week because it really helps me to understand how everything is organized and fits together. It's sort of a written meditation that prepares me for the week ahead. Also, I love to cross off the tasks by hand as I finish them.

Using this method, I can proactively catch any scheduling conflicts or potential time crunches in Step 6 and solve them *before* the week begins. This not only protects your own time and sanity, but respects the time of others you collaborate with. I go into the week with confidence that everything will be accomplished and I can smoothly work through the plan and better respond to changes as they emerge. Changes will occur; however, I do my best to stick to the plan and schedule any new happenings that arise or are requested into the following week.

Once you do this for the week, you may find that you have more open time than you thought! Now it's up to you to determine what to do with all that open time.

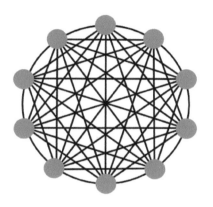

When we practice purity, we can more easily produce quality work, lead with confidence, and support ourselves and others.

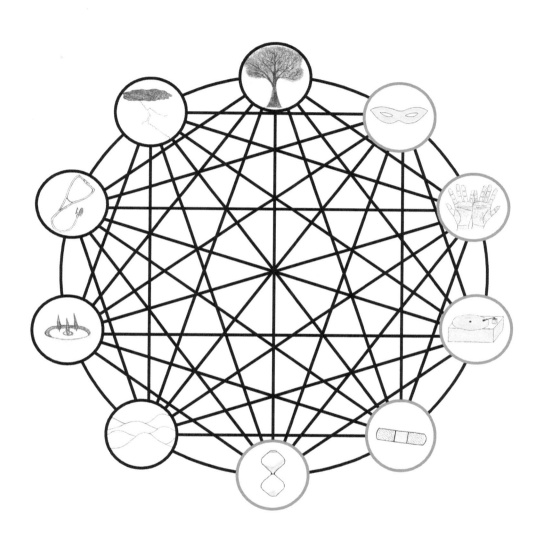

Principle 6

Contentment

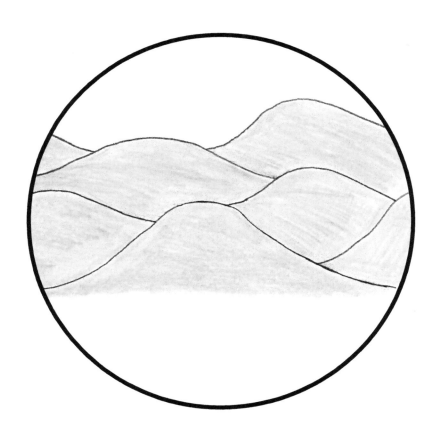

Contentment

Rising leaders have big aspirations. We're always seeking to improve and progress. When there's a constant gap between where we are and where we'd like to be, it's hard to find satisfaction. This gap in satisfaction fuels our drive but we can be hard on ourselves, which can eventually spiral into deep self doubt, anxiety, and burnout. Practicing Contentment allows us to make sustainable progress. When we practice Contentment, we slow down, zoom out, and have gratitude for our wins and learnings. We enjoy more consistent progress and wellness.

For many rising leaders, practicing contentment probably sounds counterproductive. We're supposed to be strong, productive, and pushing ourselves to the next level, right? Most rising leaders enjoy the striving part of work and leadership. The word "rising" implies an upward trajectory is happening. We often think we'd be happier if we were moving faster. However, in addition to burnout, moving too fast causes us to bypass experience and causes us to miss valuable insights.

Contentment is not about being happily settled, accepting mediocrity, or becoming stagnant. Contentment comes into the picture when we're able and willing to pause, practice gratitude, and positively acknowledge our achievements and wisdom. No matter how stagnant you may feel in a given week, acknowledging the small wins and what you're learning is progress. Contentment builds our own internal ability to foster self-confidence, which is so important in leadership. Sometimes it's beneficial for long-term progress to just observe what is and give ourselves the time to build our skills and experience. The beneficial results of Contentment allow us to reach our highest potential individually and as a team. In the Stories from the Field, we'll look at how Contentment makes us stronger as leaders and enables sustainable progress individually and collectively.

◆ ◆ ◆

Stories from the Field

1 Finding Contentment

Most of us encounter some truly humbling experiences early on in our career. I am no exception. About six months after starting my first full-time job, I felt that I had mastered it. I had learned the coding language to pull from the database, I had positive reviews from peers, and management would rely on me for information. It was getting easier to be successful each day. My confidence was building. So, I took my foot off the pedal a bit. I didn't check my work as often or as critically. I started thinking: What is next? Where can I go from here to learn the next thing?

A few weeks later, we had an important department review meeting where I presented an analysis. During the presentation, the management team found that my numbers didn't align or add up. I had made multiple mistakes. I was so embarrassed and I was really hard on myself for making the mistakes. After this experience, I'd anticipate negative feedback and was always afraid of how I would be perceived by others in meetings and interactions. I would reread an e-mail over 20 times before sending it. Making mistakes and receiving constructive feedback felt like walking on broken glass. When I sent an e-mail with a misspelling, I would agonize over it for hours afterwards. I always felt like I needed to progress faster.

My leader supported me but she also allowed me to own the mistake. This learning stayed with me. I realized that work in the real-world is always new and you always need to see with fresh eyes. Even when you feel it's easy or as though you have mastered the work, you must stay humble, patient, and awake.

When we have even a small but humbling experience, we often realize that there is always something new to learn with each project or assignment. Experiences like this call us to slow down and realize we're human. At first, slowing down is frustrating and disappointing. It takes us out of our flow. However, this is how we build strength and patience with ourselves. We can't move from experience to experience, collecting labels and milestones, without building some consistency as a professional. It's how we refine our skills and deeper understanding. It takes some longevity and dedicated focus to really excel at something.

We must acknowledge that we make mistakes and practice inner dialogue of self-support. Only true belief in ourselves can keep us going long-term. Contentment is not just about finding satisfaction and unconditional support, but about practicing gratitude for the day-to-day learnings and progress happening even when the lessons are hard to endure. The only way is through and it's easier when we allow the experiences to unfold and practice Contentment.

2 Contentment in Leadership

The most important aspect of having humbling experiences and finding contentment is that you can better relate to and support your team members.

One of my major leadership challenges, as we talked about in the Non-Stealing section, was delegating and learning to take partial or full accountability for the work of my team. As a leader, the team's work is your work and you have to take ownership over it without micromanaging it. When my team members made a mistake like an error in an e-mail or in an analysis, I would get very frustrated. My impatient, perfectionist inner critic would emerge again. I questioned if I should just do it myself and give them easier work. How would it make me look? However, I quickly learned that responding with frustration or critical comments only made my team members fearful of doing the work at all. It created animosity amongst the team. I had to change my approach in order for us to succeed. I thought about how my best leaders and mentors from my past positions had motivated me to take genuine ownership of mistakes and keep going. I realized that when there's a critical internal dialogue and your leader amplifies that negative internal dialogue, it's not only distracting but detrimental to focus and motivation.

So, I took the role of a mentor. When something went wrong or needed attention, I began offering support, encouragement, lightness and even humor to the situation. We moved faster and stayed enthusiastic. We helped each other to realize our strengths and work through struggle. By focusing on something larger than myself and practicing compassion with others, I developed compassion for myself. My work quality and stress level also improved. I balanced being diligent and detail-oriented with laughter and curiosity.

Leadership experience prompts us to shift from a mindset of self-doubt to a mindset of compassion. This helped me to sustain and progress. It helped the team to individually and collectively reach our highest potential.

All in Balance || Contentment

Contentment, if taken too far, can inhibit progress and cause us to drift. As I mentioned before, Contentment is not about finding eternal stability and consistency in our jobs. When this happens, we become stagnant and when things change, we become stressed. It is also frustrating for rising leaders.

When I was an intern, there was a period one summer when my

work stagnated. I was usually super busy but this summer was different. My leader was traveling and there were many internal organizational changes happening. At first, I kind of enjoyed the open time to do other things and not feel like I had to work overtime. However, after a few weeks, I found myself wasting time and watching the clock. As a rising leader, this got old quickly. I felt ignored. I knew I could be working on something to progress and learn but I needed direction at that point in my career. I tried practicing Contentment for a few weeks by scheduling coffee chats with different people in the company and reading industry-related articles. Finally, I knew it was time to move on. I needed a leader to facilitate that for me. I needed to find a place I would be learning, contributing, and gathering experience.

Two weeks later, once my leader returned from traveling, I had an honest conversation with him about my frustration. I was afraid of seeming annoying but I had reached the point where I needed to voice my concerns. I switched to another internal team that needed support and it was for the better. I learned a whole new skill set that has been useful throughout my career. Though it's important to allow plateau phases to come without reacting immediately, it's also important to speak up and act after a certain period to continue moving toward your highest potential. We must keep contributing to the organization, especially if we're getting paid for our time.

As leaders, how do we deal with team members that have become a little too content? I'm talking about team members that have taken Contentment too far and have become lazy or stagnant instead of motivated and aware. I once worked with a leader that had a team of enthusiastic, driven team members but also had one senior team member that never expressed interest in learning new things. He never offered to help out beyond his limited scope of work, even in situations where he was made aware that he could have been useful. He just did the minimum of what he needed to get by and often left the office early. He was great at what he did and seemed content, so the leader did not want to rock the boat. However, she also wished he would step up sometimes and help her out when additional work strained the team.

My first question to her was if he is aware of the issue and your concern. We all have the tendency to fall into patterns. If we're in the same role a long time, we can start to get comfortable with the consistency. Life happens and we don't realize when we start drifting through our days, even when the team needs us to step up. The perspective of the leader can be much different from the perspective of the individual team members, so it's important to communicate.

For this leader, it was all about making him aware and giving a call to action. By turning her frustration into an actual project for him, she structured the request for him and made it actionable. She designed and gave him a project where he would help her generate five new, amazing customer retention strategies for the following year. They met weekly for an hour and then his additional work was to brainstorm and detail new strategies each week. Instead of just meeting with him and expressing her concern with no clear direction for how to improve or change behavior, she gave a clear call to action. This structured request and framework allowed him to stay focused on his ongoing work but also prompted him to step up and help her in a new way that leveraged his skills and expertise. It was a balance of patience and encouragement toward higher potential for him individually and for the team. As leaders, we must encourage our team members to remain content but also action-oriented.

Reflection

What is a challenging or humbling transformative experience you have had personally or professionally? How did it change your perspective and the way you work?

_____

_____

_____

_____

How can you reframe that transformative experience as a win? What did you learn from that experience that you will take forward to improve your journey and share with your team?

_____

_____

_____

_____

What wisdom do you feel like you're currently gaining at work? – Not only hard skills and achievements but deeper skills and wisdom that take patience and strategic thinking to master?

_____

_____

_____

_____

Action

Exercise 1: Weekly Wins

Why? Acknowledging wins builds confidence, enthusiasm, and gratitude.

Contentment is about gratitude, patience, and compassion. When we pause and reflect on our achievements, we feel more accomplished and grateful. We see how we are progressing and evolving even during weeks where it may feel stagnant from time to time. When we zoom out and look at the week as a whole, we can see where true progress happened. If you keep track of this each week, it can become a reference for your resume or interview prep. This can also serve as a means of measuring when you may be too content - when is it time to ask for a new challenging project or experience?

Reflect on the week: the meetings, the projects, and the conversations and try to write down at least 3 wins from this week. They can be things you did independently or as part of a team. Use the space below or a journal to jot down your wins from this week. If this is beneficial for you, put a calendar reminder on your schedule to do this weekly. I like to do this exercise on Fridays.

Weekly Wins

_____

_____

_____

_____

Exercise 2: Weekly Wisdom

Why? Acknowledging wisdom builds gratitude and enthusiasm.

This exercise allows you to pause and acknowledge the wisdom you've gained. It develops an attitude of gratitude and collaboration. Expressing gratitude may seem soft but pausing to do this weekly helps to cultivate Contentment. It also keeps us accountable for gaining wisdom and staying aware of it! Wisdom goes well beyond just what you put on your resume. Wisdom can include new skills, knowledge, insights, or, most importantly, deeper understanding about someone or something based on your experience. Sometimes it seems that the grass is always greener on the other side or, as we saw in Stories from the Field I, we move too quickly through things and this can cause burnout and errors.

You can record your Weekly Wisdom along with your Weekly Wins on Fridays. Use the space below or a journal and jot down pieces of wisdom you have gained this week. If this is beneficial for you, put a calendar reminder on your schedule weekly.

Weekly Wisdom

_____

_____

_____

_____

Acknowledging the small wins and what you're learning - even while going through a plateau period - is progress.

You are **always** learning something.

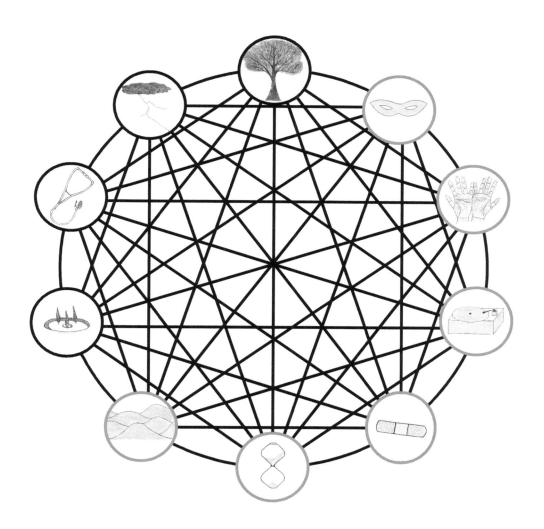

Principle 7

Discipline

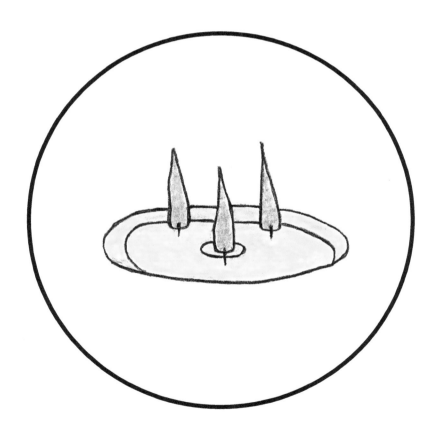

Discipline

As we continue on our ethical path, we have now prepared ourselves for the challenging yet rewarding practice of Discipline. Here, we talk mainly in terms of self-discipline. Self-discipline is an ethical practice that takes our personal and professional development to the next level. As curious, driven leaders, we often have deep-rooted self-discipline practices from our educational and professional training. We know that we should follow through with what we signed up for and pledged to do. However, in the face of new, intense challenges or disappointments, we can often find ourselves off track and making excuses for why we don't want to complete something we intended to do. How do we stay motivated to follow through even when it seems impossible or we find ourselves looking for a way out? How do we know when it is right to back out of an experience versus stay strong and continue?

In the ancient system, this principle literally refers to an inner fire. We have to cultivate a deep inner fire within ourselves to work through challenging situations. To practice Discipline is to keep the inner fire of curiosity, motivation, and action going in order to show up each day and follow through with projects you've started.

Why is discipline an ethical practice? If we want to back out of something that is a challenge, why go through the effort? If we don't feel like doing something, why do it? Discipline is ethical because it is how we transform toward our highest potential. Challenge and struggle can serve as our wisest teachers. When we motivate ourselves and go to our edge, pushing ourselves a little further than we normally may, a bit beyond our comfort zone, we often learn the most. We learn more about our strengths, our likes and dislikes, and more about the human experience that is so important to understand as a leader.

In my experience, discipline has been rewarding even just to experience the spectrum of emotions – from struggle, to excitement, to ease. Through struggle often comes blissful periods of ease and realizations that you may not have come across had you not followed through with a challenge. Discipline involves keeping that internal fire strong so you continue to show up for yourself and your team. Even on the hard days, each day is a day to learn, grow stronger, and transform. In the exercises, we'll practice ways to keep the inner fire of motivation and curiosity alive.

◆ ◆ ◆

Stories from the Field

1 - My First Lesson in Discipline

Transitioning departments within a company is not as easy as it may seem. Early in my career, I was given the opportunity to move from one department to another. Making a transition within the company means that it is not your typical two weeks notice. Upon accepting the offer for the new position, the leadership team decided that I would remain in my current analyst position until a replacement for my position was found – no timeline given. They had to go through the hiring process and find a replacement for my current position before I could move on. Fortunately, I loved my analytics manager and the team. Unfortunately, our analytics director didn't respond so well when I officially gave my notice. The day following the notice discussion with my manager, the director asked to meet with me. We walked outside, both silent toward the river, and I felt my breath getting shorter and shallower. Was she going to throw me in the river? She looked around and then at me, paused, and said that I'd made the biggest mistake of my career. She said that I'd regret it later on for not sticking with this opportunity and there was nothing we could do now but I should really think about the decision I had made and learn from it. I was scared. We walked back inside and I left early to go home.

I then proceeded to have the awkward situation of sitting next to my director each day at the office until a replacement was found. No miracle happened right away. For about eight weeks, I continued to show up. Each day, I checked with my manager on how the recruiting process was going in finding my replacement. The glares and nervous energy from my director kept me up at night, literally. I felt like she was going to explode at me at any moment throughout the day. My manager offered to switch desks with me so there would be a buffer. I did not know how to resolve this awkward situation aside from showing up each day and doing my best, trusting the universe that I would eventually be able to move on.

After a few weeks of feeling as though they would never find someone to fill my role, I decided to get real. If I didn't have control over my path, what was next? What was Plan B? Should I abandon it all together? I realized that I was showing up because I was looking forward to moving on to my next position. Giving up would mean that I would have to give up the offer for my next position as well. This was plan A, B, C, and Z. I wanted to experience this next role. I knew it was the right thing to do. If the days were so hard and so stressful, why not use my vacation time now? Why not "get sick" for a few days and get my space? I realized that I was also showing up for my current manager and the team. I could have gone on sick leave (since, during a lot of this period, I actually was) but I felt the relationship was important to me. I still found some joy in coming in to work each day, despite the uncomfortable situation. It felt like a long summer but, finally, by the end of the summer, someone accepted my position and I moved on to my new role. I think every muscle in my body released and I slept 15 hours the night I heard the news about the new hire. It was, in a way, bittersweet at that point to leave my analytics manager I loved so much. We had somewhat bonded even more over that tough transition period. However, I moved on to my new position to take on a really exciting new project.

In hindsight, during the transition period, I was able to observe the contrast between my director and my manager. When I became a leader, I used the contrast between how my manager and how my director reacted to my departure as an example of how to and how not to lead. The director was only hurting herself and the team performance by scolding me and creating an environment of fear. It was about how each made me feel and how each reaction impacted the potential of the team. I realized how unnecessarily awkward even seasoned leaders can make situations and how it hurts the team morale in many ways. I already respected my manager but my admiration and respect for her grew during that period of support.

I soon learned that the discipline - the ability to deeply connect to my intention - and the strength I had built during that experience would come in handy in my new position. The new position was not easy. I learned not only the value of discipline but also how to handle challenging situations and what my triggers and limits are, mentally and physically. By pursuing new challenges and following through, you learn your own limits and you build strength to surpass them.

2 - Discipline as a Leader

As a leader, it is often a challenge to keeping the team momentum going. When everything is smooth and exciting, people show up enthusiastically, diligently complete their work, and participate. On the other hand, there are times when work is slow, someone goes through a rough period personally, or organizational changes happen and the positive energy, motivation, and discipline have to be cultivated internally by the leader. This means motivating not only yourself but also motivating your team even when the going gets hard.

I served as a leader through a rough reorganization in a large corporation and there were weeks where it was challenge to keep the team engaged. It's funny how deadlines do not change even when organizational chaos strikes. My team was often distracted and discouraged by layoff announcements and urgent requests. I found myself getting off the path, too. I realized that I needed to step it up. We were drifting and we were only getting more behind each day. Many leaders resort to designing incentives and consequences so that team members stay motivated. However, from experience, I knew that using carrots to incentivize team members was not sustainable and created an environment of fear and animosity. Instead, I found that discipline could be cultivated naturally.

There are five key practices that contributed to smoother teamwork and cultivated team discipline during this period of chaos. The first piece is staying tethered to our mission and intentions as a team. I made Monday and Friday team meetings, even if just for 15 minutes each, a priority. We reviewed our team's vision and task list together and I made sure team priorities were clear. The second is ritual – both personal and team rituals. I added at least one team get-together each month for lunch or an offsite trip. I led in-office activities also when people needed breaks. I had my own rituals that grounded me day-to-day. You'll reflect on your own in the exercises. The third piece is support. I made sure to constantly ask my team if they had the resources they needed and felt the workload was manageable. I emphasized positive reinforcement of their work. The fourth is leading by example. As a leader, it's even more important to lead by example and show up through the good and hard times. This is where self-discipline comes in. It's challenging to remain engaged and curious about what you're learning and creating, especially in the most mundane or tedious times. However, as a leader, you are a mirror for the team in many ways. It's true. As we talked about in Control of Energy, they gauge your energy and motivation. When I'd show up by 8am, the team would as well. Finally, the fifth is rest. This is my fuel for leading by example and supporting the team. I began using more of my weekend time to rejuvenate. Many leaders don't take rest, so it's actually a discipline practice to make sure you get your rest so you can do your best work!

We all need encouragement at times and this can serve as gentle discipline in itself. A responsibility of a leader is to keep the team tethered to and enthusiastic about the vision. Forcing motivation through incentives and consequences is not sustainable. You have to authentically tether your team to the vision and lead by example. It will feel more effortless and sustainable for your team and for you. When the leader practices self-discipline, it naturally cultivates discipline amongst the team.

◆ ◆ ◆

All in Balance || Discipline

Sometimes the internal fire of Discipline gets too strong. We come into work highly motivated and excited to see how far we can go. We take on too much or push ourselves or our team too far. What happens when we have too much fire? We often burn out or burn our teams out. This happens to many high-achieving leaders and teams.

Since Discipline is about building strength, it makes sense that we shouldn't push it too far. When we physically push our body too far, we break something, pull something, etc. We have to alternate challenge with rest and integration. Make sure you find that balance of effort and ease that allows you to build new strength but also keep your consistent progress going toward the vision. You can always back out of the fire but that doesn't mean you have to give up. It's about going to your edge but realizing when you need to back off. Keep showing up. When I was faced with situations that were challenging, uncomfortable, or difficult, I would often have doubt and think: if this is so uncomfortable, should I not be doing it? However, sometimes discomfort is not the best indication that you should pull out of something. Discomfort is often how you build awareness and strength. I'm not suggesting you torture yourself, but intentionally pushing to new limits is how we grow and gain confidence. Some of my deepest growth has come from showing up when it seemed almost impossible.

Also, I had difficulty finding the discipline to stop working and take rest. I have found that when I take breaks, I return rejuvenated and work much more efficiently. However, when I get into the flow of work and people are actively communicating and requesting help, it takes discipline to define the line and take time away from work. Short breaks periodically help keep energy and focus optimal and longer vacation rest breaks help fuel creativity. When we take time away, we return with new ideas and energy.

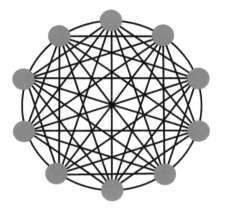

Reflection

Is there a time where you faced a challenge and found it difficult to follow through? What motivation helped you to follow through or what ultimately caused you to not follow through?

_____

_____

_____

_____

What keeps your inner fire going day-to-day currently? Why do you show up for work?

_____

_____

_____

_____

How do you cultivate discipline on your team? How do you provide motivation for progress?

_____

_____

_____

_____

Action

Exercise 1: Writing Your Mission Statement

Why? Gain clarity on your core mission - your actions and the true impacts they make for the customer, audience, or end user to naturally cultivate discipline to move forward.

When we are tethered to a clear mission we can remain clear and motivated about what we're showing up to accomplish each day. A mission statement answers the questions: What do you do? What is your contribution to and impact on the organization? What is your impact on the end-user or customer? Why do you do what you do, really - at a personal fulfillment level, right now?

The best part about developing a mission statement is that you really get down to the root reason of why you're doing what you're doing or setting out to do. At the end of the day (or every hour, on crazy days), you can look back at the mission and return to why you're really doing what you're doing: why you decided to embark on this specific way to move toward your highest potential. I also designed a method for writing a team mission statement which is detailed in the Awake Leadership guidebook. This personal mission statement is similar in terms of purpose but done a bit differently to serve at the individual level.

When we have a mission, discipline becomes more effortless because the path becomes clear and there is motivation to reach the end of the tunnel. This statement is a personal mission statement for you to keep as a reminder and driver for self-discipline. A statement like this helped me immensely in the case of Story from the Field 1.

Exercise 1: Writing Your Mission Statement

Prompt 1: Define Your What, Define the Actions

Many people say start with why. However, it's sometimes too hard to start with why - we need to start with what we're doing right now. For some reason, what we're doing right now it the best solution for us, right? Maybe we know something else is out there we could be doing but for a big reason or many, what we're doing right now is optimal. We may also have prospects for work we're deciding about. What are you doing day-to-day or setting out to do? What projects, objectives, or milestones have you set out to achieve recently?

_____

_____

_____

_____

_____

_____

_____

Action

Exercise 1: Writing Your Mission Statement

Prompt 2: Define the Why, Define the Impact on the Organization

How do your actions day-to-day and what you contribute through your work impact the organization? Why does the organization ask you to do what you do? What do you contribute? What outcomes or key metrics do you impact?

_____

_____

_____

_____

_____

_____

_____

Exercise 1: Writing Your Mission Statement

Prompt 3: Define the Why, Define the Impact on the World

How do your actions day-to-day and what you contribute through your work impact the end-users or customers? Even if it is once-removed, outline that here. How does your work day-to-day, your actions, shape the customer or end-user's experience?

_____

_____

_____

_____

_____

_____

_____

Action

Exercise 1: Writing Your Mission Statement

Prompt 4: Define your Why, Identify your Core Motivation

What aspects of this work (current or prospective) excite you? Why do you get up everyday to achieve these objectives and do this work? This is your deeper why. There are many core reasons we do what we do. However, many of us get stuck on the surface of looking for acknowledgement and achievement. Examples of deeper whys are cultivating connections with people, supporting your family, the ability to learn and travel, freedom and flexibility in your schedule.

_____

_____

_____

_____

_____

_____

_____

Exercise 1: Writing Your Mission Statement

Examples of personal mission statements:

◆ My mission is to complete project A this year in order to cultivate deeper connections with like-minded people and expand my network.

◆ My mission is to reach my position targets this year in order to be considered for a promotion and expand my realm of responsibility and learning potential.

◆ My mission is to meet the three key objectives my leader has set for me in order to receive my maximum bonus and invest in traveling somewhere new with my family.

You may realize the part before "in order to" is the what and the part after "in order to" is the why.

My mission is to _____(actions from Prompt 1)_____ **in order to**

_____(deeper whys from prompts 2, 3, and/or 4)_____.

The space below is for your Mission Statement drafting practice.

_____

_____

_____

_____

Action

Exercise 2: Rituals for Discipline

Why? Rituals serve as a supportive structure for getting our work done to achieve the mission. They also give us things to look forward to each day and give us a consistent platform for measuring progress and change.

Rituals are especially important when the going gets tough. Rituals should be designed to support your mission day-to-day as you follow through. I like the word ritual over routine because ritual implies intention; that you have awareness and a clear reason you're doing everything you do. Routines are good but they can become meaningless, autopilot, and lazy. Rituals are meaningful and intentional. Rituals also provide a consistent path from where you can see progress emerge. When you have a white canvas and, each week, you paint a bit more, the newness emerges on that consistent platform. Rituals provide something for people to look forward to even when the work is uncertain. Rituals help you to find flow in your day-to-day.

For me, my morning ritual is my consistent practice of self-discipline that sets the tone for the day. When I wake up, do my morning exercises and meditation, make my oatmeal and coffee, and then sit down to write, I can gauge my energy day-to-day. I see progress on my writing and personal experience as well. I start the day with a self-discipline practice I enjoy and it puts the day in motion.

Exercise 2: Rituals for Discipline

The Prompt: Your Rituals

What personal rituals support you day-to-day? What rituals do you look forward to that enable you to show up to work feeling energetic and focused or to conclude your day peacefully?

_____

_____

_____

_____

_____

_____

_____

When we go further toward our edge, beyond our comfort zone, we often learn the most. We build strength and gain wisdom.

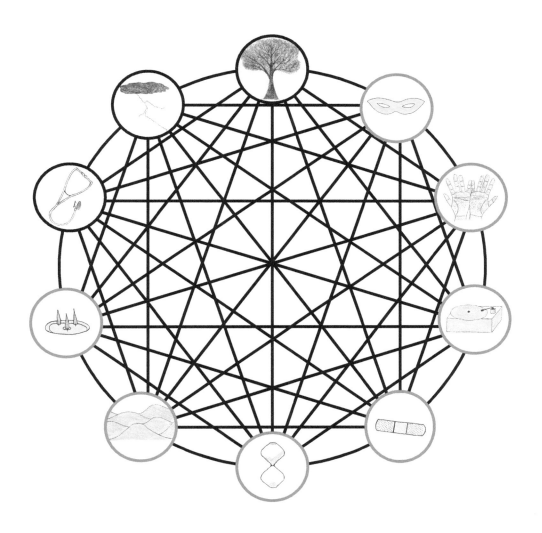

Principle 8

Self-Study

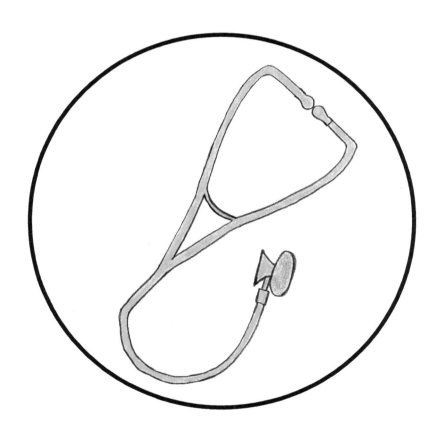

Self-Study

The ethical practices of Purity, Contentment, and Discipline toward ourselves set us up perfectly for the deeper practice of Self-Study. We need to utilize all three of the preceding ethical practices toward ourselves to successfully practice Self-Study. To study is to devote time and attention to a subject or topic of investigation. Studying involves looking closely at something to observe it and better understand it. Through studying, we become aware, gain knowledge, and understand something better. We expand our awareness. When we understand something, we then better know how to utilize it or how to change it. In school, we study things that help us understand how the world works and focus on specific topics and skills that will be useful in our future work and life. However, we're rarely given a class in Self-Study and rarely take the time to practice it.

For the purposes of Awake Ethics, I'll focus on Self-Study with respect to leadership. Self-Study is not just about anatomy or psychology. Self-Study is the practice of studying our strengths, our behaviors, our mindset, and our preferences. By spending time reflecting and understanding these aspects of ourselves, we can become more confident and move forward on our path more efficiently and with more clarity. When we practice Self-Study, we develop the ability to leverage our strengths and know how we want to change and evolve to progress forward on our path. We study and understand how we connect and add value to the world. It's a continuous, iterative practice because we're constantly changing.

Self-Study is ultimately how we transform and move further toward our highest potential. It helps us to understand our assumptions and perspective about ourselves. It's how we break out of stagnant robot mode and into the unique, one-of-kind, authentic version of ourselves. Some may say this is like self-awareness but it's deeper than that. Self-awareness is something we practice in the moment. Through Self-Study, we become clear about our values and about why we do what we do. It is how we develop confidence and authenticity in our leadership, which helps in supporting and motivating our teams. As leaders, confidence is key, but it must be genuinely cultivated. I have found that this can only be accomplished through Self-Study... and it's an ongoing effort!

Whether you're working to discover what you excel at, what you want to do, or you're working to develop more confidence, Self-Study is the practice that will get you there. Let's take a look at it in practice.

Stories from the Field

1 - Observe, Reflect, and Rewire

As many do, I started Self-Study at a time when I needed solutions. During my first role as manager of a large project, I often felt exhausted and stressed. This anxiety was affecting my work in that I'd cancel meetings or forget things easily. On days when I didn't feel stressed and exhausted, I could produce more work, follow through on meetings I had scheduled, and would come up with many new ideas. I knew this because there were weeks where I felt on top of my game. However, in this new role, I often felt the burnout. I couldn't focus and contribute my best work. This perpetual feeling of exhaustion and anxiety was something I recognized before but never solved. I had never asked why I felt this way; I just accepted it and pushed through until I reached a high point again. My usual response to feeling tired and stressed was to drink a cup of coffee, get through the work day, return home even more tired, watch TV, and fall asleep. I would call friends or family members and they'd encourage me on my way and advise that I keep working hard. Finally, I realized that I needed sustainable answers to the issues that were keeping me from feeling my best, or at least at peace day-to-day.

The first step was developing awareness of the root cause of the stress. What was I resisting and why? Through writing daily just for 20 minutes each morning, I started to observe and reflect on the previous day or previous few days and what my environment was like on days when I didn't feel at my best. These were often days that resulted in stress, frustration, or exhaustion.

We all have struggles. However, when the negative impacts felt chronic and as though they were keeping me from my highest potential, I needed to resolve them to move forward. I needed to move toward feeling my best so I could contribute my best. I continued writing and asked myself: Why do I feel this way after these specific instances that are such "normal" aspects of the working world happen? I continued writing and reflecting to really get down to what specifically was causing my lack of motivation.

By continuing to ask why, I found:

◆ On days when I had multiple meetings with heated discussion, I felt exhausted
◆ On days when meetings were scheduled over my lunch break and I skipped taking a break for lunch, I felt depleted
◆ When I impulsively reacted too quickly to new requests and inquiries that came in to my e-mail inbox, I'd feel tired
◆ On days when I didn't have a to-do list for the day I'd feel unprepared
◆ When I received many urgent e-mails or requests throughout the day, I'd feel nervous

When I realized that these were the potential triggers, I already felt better. I could change my habits and behaviors to start to resolve the negative feelings and anxiety. With this understanding, I could now question what I could do to reframe my mindset and relation to it, or change my environment.

Based on my findings, I rewired or changed my behavior in a few different ways. First, during meetings with heated discussion, I became a listener. I was fully there and participated but instead of reacting to everything that was said, I took the witness perspective. I rewired my default response from knee-jerk and over eager to listener and thoughtful participant. I made my default to listen instead of to respond, unless I had something unique and highly valuable to add to the discussion.

I also protected my personal time during the day. I blocked off my time for lunch and didn't allow meetings to get scheduled over it. I would take the time to read, take a walk, or go off-site for lunch. Third, instead of running out of the office when I was finished my work for the day, I started to always set aside 15 or 20 minutes at the end of the day to make my to-do list and schedule for the next day. I learned that, for me, time spent planning is time well spent. I can flow through the next day more easily and also have more capacity to respond to new requests, and know how to prioritize.

Finally, in terms of the urgent emails and requests, instead of just shutting off my email all the time, I rewired my reaction, or created a system where I would read the e-mail when it arrived and if it wasn't a same-day need, I would file it away to read at the end of the day. This meant I would only immediately respond to about 1 out of 10 e-mails. I'd respond to operational e-mails and also questions from my team members. If I was doing an analysis or project that needed dedicated focus, I would shut down my e-mail for up to one hour after letting my team know.

Making these small but impactful changes in behavior gave me new, more consistent vitality. These were sustainable solutions that I still use today. By studying my own mindset and behaviors, I was able to create more optimal conditions for my best work. I rewired my reactions and my conditions to mitigate stress and burnout. All of these were life-changing improvements that came from Self-Study, not from a manager or leader telling me that I had to do these things. I was able to move toward a more authentic, enjoyable way of working that also improved the quality of work I provide for others. However, as you'll see in the next section, sometimes bigger changes are necessary.

2 - Truthfulness and Self-Study

When was the last time you felt prepared for an interview? They're hard for the interviewee and hard for employers, too. It's almost impossible to know how someone will actually perform in the role by spending just a few sessions with them. It's impossible for the candidate to know for sure if they'll really enjoy the role. There's a lot of uncertainty. Sometimes candidates are very vetted and spend a lot of time with the prospective employer so that their skills and qualities can show through. However, with more entry-level positions, it's often just one or two conversations before a decision is made. This is why self-knowledge and truthfulness with others during interview conversations are so important. For eager candidates, it's easy to exaggerate in interviews. We also often give in to circumstances or job functions that really don't align with our desires.

When working on a small technical team, we were told one day that they'd finally hired our new director. We were told that she had the perfect experience for the role and she'd have amazing new ideas and skills to share with us. When she started, she shared a lot of great team activities and we all felt more in synch. She clearly had strengths. However, once we got to the execution part and needed her to review our analytical work, she didn't seem to be able to advise us. There was a lot she didn't know. Over time, it became clear that she was very insecure in submitting project work to her leader because she wasn't quite sure how to check our team's work for accuracy. After a few months, she admitted to us that she didn't understand a lot of the technical things we were doing. I wondered if she'd been honest in her interview about her technical knowledge. For a while, I was frustrated. Then I felt a little sorry for her. I realized that she was now in a tough position. She lasted a little while longer but was soon let go.

If you know yourself and if you are truthful about who you are - your strengths, your experience, and your interests - you'll always be prepared for interviews and things will work out for the best. You'll ask the right questions and move in a more authentic direction along your path. You can still aim high; taking positions a bit beyond our experience gives us room to grow and learn. However, be honest with yourself and your potential employer about your strengths, interests, knowledge, and experience. It will set you free and set you up for success in reaching your highest potential.

◆ ◆ ◆

All in Balance || Self-Study

When we become obsessed with Self-Study, it can actually lead to stress from overanalyzing everything. Do you really need to know exactly how many calories you should consume each day given your physical exertion? What is our best? When are we feeling great? Though it is fun to try and have exact answers to these questions, there is much about ourselves that we'll never completely understand. The mystery is healthy, I have found. We can burn out from too much Self-Study. Make sure to take time to relax and just be content when possible. It takes time.

Seek to understand what you love to do and what makes you feel the way you want to feel. We're so quick to call for help or to numb ourselves out when we don't feel at our best or when we can't solve a problem. Instead of numbing out or instantly calling for help, try practicing patience and be the witness to your own feelings and reactions. It doesn't always take a specialist or professional to tell you what's wrong. Take input from others but then reflect on your own truths based on your own experience. When you practice Self-Study, you discover underlying, unbiased truths about yourself and you can then truly understand the why behind your mindset and behaviors. It's not just about solving one thing you identify today; it's about learning a life-long practice of problem solving and overcoming personal and professional obstacles as they arise. Self-Study is a skill that leads toward transformation and toward your highest potential. It helps to find the environments, people, and work that fuel our best feelings and best contributions. This practice is also important for leadership because it builds confidence. When we prove to ourselves that we're not a victim of our circumstances or our conditioning, we gain the power to truly understand ourselves and our mindset. We then also have the knowledge and confidence to change it.

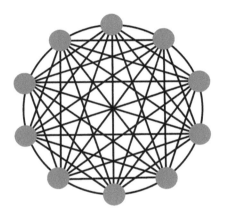

What is your way of practicing Self-Study? How do you pause, reflect, and move forward with clarity and more authenticity? (For example: writing, walks, exercise, time in nature, ...)

_____

_____

_____

_____

How do you feel on your best days? What are five words to describe how you feel on your best days at work and in life?

_____

_____

_____

_____

When do you not feel at your best? What are the key feelings and also, if you can identify them, what are the triggers that lead up to feeling this way? How do these triggers and feelings keep you from moving toward your highest potential?

_____

_____

_____

_____

Action

Exercise 1: Strengths Finder

Why? Reflecting on our strengths through structured exercises is a good spring board for beginning to realize our strengths and for further reflecting on our strengths and interests.

Self-Study is about observation and reflection. There are tools that can help us discover our strengths, weaknesses, and interests. This type of exercise is a perfect example for how to kick-start the practice of Self-Study. The Strengths Finder 2.0 test tells you your five primary strengths based on a detailed online questionnaire.

I take the Strengths Finder 2.0 test every year as a reflection point for observing how my strengths, according to this benchmark, change and progress. It's really interesting to see how the results change (or don't) each year. I have found that they have become more consistent as I have aged, played to my strengths in terms of the work I do, and found a better work-life balance.

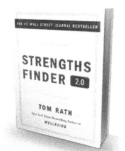

Step 1: Purchase Book and Quiz

Purchase the StrengthsFinder 2.0 books on Amazon or from the Gallup website. There is a unique access code (in the back of the book) to take the strengths assessment online.

Step 2: Take the Quiz

Using the code in the back of your book, go to the Gallup website and take the assessment independently. It takes about 30 - 45 minutes. Once you have taken the test, download your PDF with your five primary strengths.

Exercise 1: Strengths Finder 2.0

Step 3: Reflect on the Results

Read about each of your five strengths. Do they ring true to you? Once you have reviewed your results, answer the reflection questions below.

Which of your five strengths resonate most - which are not surprising to you? Why?

_____

_____

_____

Which of your five strengths don't resonate - which are surprising or counter to what you perceive your strengths to be? Why?

_____

_____

_____

How could you further leverage these strengths in your work to accomplish your vision and objectives?

_____

_____

_____

Action

Exercise 2: Studying the Work of Others

Why? Other people give us inspiration. Others serve as a means for seeing what we are not or don't want to aspire to be like as leaders.

Is there a certain influencer you have that you work with or follow? What do you admire about him or her? What qualities do you see in yourself and what qualities do you aspire to cultivate and why?

This exercise may seem like studying others, not Self-Study. However, when we think about who we aspire to be like, who we study, and who we follow and why, we learn a lot about ourselves in turn. We also begin to observe and learn how we are different from the rest. It's best to study a range of different leaders and influencers. No one single leader or influencer is you!

Begin with the prompts on the following pages.

Exercise 2: Studying the Work of Others

What leader or influencer do you follow or aspire to be like? Why?

_____

_____

_____

_____

Why do you follow them or study with them? What contributions have they made or qualities do they have that you admire or aspire to?

_____

_____

_____

_____

Action

Exercise 2: Studying the Work of Others

What attributes or vibe do they emanate that you would like to aspire to as well? Use specific descriptor words or point out specific behaviors or examples.

_____

_____

_____

_____

What do you learn from them?

_____

_____

_____

_____

Note (to Self): Read!

Reading books by leaders of companies and organizations you admire will give you new insights into what makes others confident and successful on their terms. Many great leaders now share their stories through biographies or online publications. Pick up a biography of someone you believe has an interesting story or has started a successful company or organization. Gain inspiration for forging your own path and learn from them!

Exercise 3: Daily Writing

Why? Writing daily gives us a consistent, clean, simple platform for reflecting on our approach, mindset, and progress.

Here is my favorite exercise: writing, of course. Just like Mind Mapping, an Awake guidebook would not be complete without suggesting daily writing. This exercise is adapted from *The Artist's Way* by Julia Cameron.

Keep a journal of your day-to-day as I did in Story from the Field 1. By starting with how you feel each day, you're cultivating this practice of awareness and Self-Study. Document the events of the day and how they translate to those feelings. Awareness is the foundation for change and authentic progress.

If you write daily for 20 minutes, it will become a ritual and you'll begin to see the benefits for starting the day with this practice. I suggest doing this when you first get up in the morning, when your mind is calm and the world is most fresh. Whether you need to prep and organize your thoughts for the day, resolve something on your mind, or give yourself a pep talk, this practice is a game-changer. Once you start free writing, it usually takes about 5 - 10 minutes to break the ice, so don't give up! Just start. You may even start to look forward to it!

By practicing Self-Study, we become more confident and aware. We move forward with more clarity and authenticity.

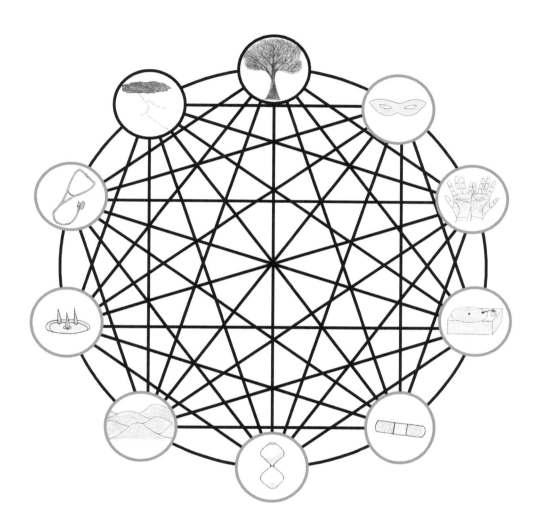

Surrender

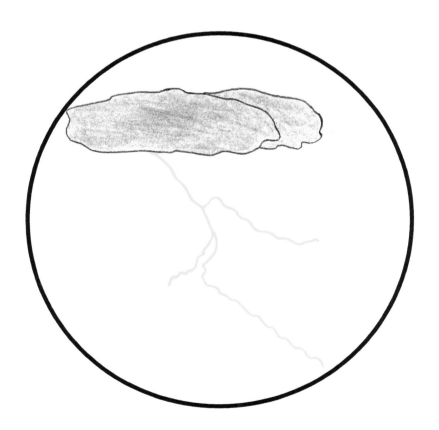

Surrender

The best opportunities for growth and progress often arise when we let go of things that don't serve us. Surrender is the second phase of Non-Attachment. Once we let go of the expectations or old perceptions that no longer serve us, we must look for and embrace the opportunities that follow. To do this, we must acknowledge that we do not have total control over the direction of our team or our path, especially when working in medium and large organizations.

In the ancient system, the principle of Surrender refers to surrendering to a higher power to allow, accept, and embrace what life offers. We'll keep much of that original interpretation here because can't we all agree that ultimately we don't have control over everything? There are always unknowns and unexpected phenomena that arise. On the bright side, not having total control means that life often offers new possibility and gifts to us that we could not plan for.

In business, we're conditioned to maintain control over our team and responsibilities. We are very familiar with practicing Surrender in our personal lives but in business, where we're held accountable for our work and bringing a planned vision to reality, we hold tight to the plan. Control is a skill we're evaluated on. However, in the grand scheme of things, especially in large organizations, we have little control given the complex, interdependent nature of organizations.

Surrender doesn't suggest that we should come in everyday to go through the motions and blame our mistakes on other people or on the universe. We do have control over many aspects of our day-to-day progress. Surrender suggests that we let go of aspects that we often stress over and relentlessly try to control, to give us more freedom to focus on the areas that we can control and are truly responsible for. This gives us more time to focus on our strengths, to make impactful progress, and to enjoy our work more. As we'll see in the Stories from the Field, opportunities to Surrender arise at often unexpected moments in unexpected ways. Surrendering offers us new possibilities to progress toward our highest potential individually and as a team.

◆　◆　◆

Stories from the Field

1 - Identity

As high-achieving leaders, we often get attached to a certain vision and path for how we want our career to unfold. Sometimes we're given the grand vision by our leader or our parents. Sometimes we create the vision for ourselves. I was always working to create an identity for myself and designing who I wanted to be in 10, 20, or 30 years. This can be good in that it provides direction and vision. Vision helps with discipline and decision-making. However, when we give ourselves a certain identity or attach to a certain, specific long-term path of expectations and desires, we put a lot of pressure on ourselves and often miss out on great opportunities that arise along the way. We must learn this important practice of Surrendering to what our heart says and the universe offers.

I absolutely loved my first job. I loved the creative people at the company, the visual aspect of the offices and the lively vibe. I loved participating in the process of bringing the product to life. I was a part of it and it was a part of me. However, there came a point, after about three years, when I felt that the environment had developed into a place that was not supportive for my health, my development, and my relationships. These were all things that had started to occur to me but my job still came first. I was attached. I blamed my unhappiness on the new hires and the harsh winters. I thought it was just a phase. However, days became more difficult and my health started to suffer.

I knew that I needed a change but I also truly felt that the company wouldn't survive without me. I had tightly woven the whole thing - the whole package of the job, the community, the vibe - into my identity. Who would I be without it? It was, after all, the place I spent most of my time each day and it was my primary focus. I had even carefully crafted my own title. Who would I be without my title? What would I tell people about myself when I was out to dinner? This was my identity. I was resistant to acknowledging that it was even an option to leave. While I was holding on, this ethical system came into my life. The ethical principle of Surrender was staring me in the face.

At first I was closed off to relating this new learning to what was going on in my life day-to-day. It took months for me to realize that everything happens for a reason, including this learning. One day, I was flipping back through my daily writing and realized that though I had done everything I could to reframe my mindset and adapt, the environment was no longer for me. It was an environment of animosity and it was not fueling my best work. We had grown apart in many ways. However, I was attached to this place as part of my identity and I feared who I would or wouldn't be without it. I didn't have another option. I finally went through enough introspection and suffering to continuously find myself asking why I was continuing to do what I was doing. Was this leading toward my highest potential when I felt so confused and empty?

What was really stopping me? Through more introspection, time alone, and writing, I realized that I feared not being a somebody. I feared having to reconstruct my day-to-day from scratch that I had worked so hard to create. I feared having to reconstruct who I was and what I did. I feared an identity void. I feared judgment. I also felt horrible and really stuck. What would I do if I wasn't doing this? How would I survive? Who would I be?

First, I had to practice Non-Attachment. I had to separate my identity from this place and detach from the notion that my survival was contingent on it. I could find another job. It had turned into something that I was not. I had turned into something that it was not. I was no longer doing my best work, my heart wasn't in it, and it was time to go. Our collaboration was no longer leading either of us toward our highest potential.

It took a lot of writing and persuading myself to trust that the company would be okay without me and I would be okay without it. In addition to letting go, I committed to trusting the larger picture - the universe, if you will. Once I trusted that there would be other options and a better path waiting for me, I opened up. I became curious instead of afraid. The combination of Non-Attachment and Surrender allowed me to open to new possibilities. I applied for new jobs and connected with old contacts. I remained open to receive what came back in terms of interest and opportunities. Some opportunities I applied for worked out and some did not. As the universe would have it, six months later, I was in a new role, with a new title, in a new desk 3,000 miles away and feeling much healthier. My previous employer was fine too. I gained confidence in my intuition and ability to let go and trust.

Practicing Non-Attachment and Surrender opens opportunity for transformation. It takes persistence and trust. Surrender is the ultimate trust test: trusting the universe is there to catch you. It's a trapeze transition. You have to persuade yourself to let go of that grip, which is usually the mind holding on more than your heart and your hands. It takes letting go of ego and what people tell you is right or successful. Ultimately, only you and the universe can be your best teachers and advisors. Surrender is freedom and flexibility. When we practice Surrender, we welcome new opportunity.

2 - Cross-Functional Projects

Whenever we do something new, we take a risk. There are unknowns. This is a common challenge for leaders of growing companies and organizations. As a project planner and manager, I had my first true leadership experience in Surrender.

I gave direction for new projects and initiatives and determined how they should be planned and executed. Whenever we must advise about how to approach or do something new, we make assumptions based on the past as well as our knowledge and instincts.

Some projects I managed involved forecasting and planning for retail products and for workforce (people) needs and costs. As you can imagine, forecasting and planning around physical goods was much easier and predictable than controlling the patterns and costs of labor. I learned to model scenarios based on what I could not control or predict. Turnover is not easy to forecast and it depends on many factors.

Many people I have worked with closely know that one of my favorite phrases I use often is "plan the work and work the plan". However, the reality is that things don't always go according to the plan. No matter how meticulously you plan the work, unexpected things come up, especially in large collaborative projects. When you're working out in the field, nothing is exactly like something done before and the outcome is never certain. Unexpected things always arise along the way. I was afraid because there was uncertainty but I realized that if I focused on the aspects I could control and kept a positive, solution-centric attitude, I could stick to the plan and respond to change. I learned to give it my best shot and looked forward to watching how things actually unfolded.

Surrender involves taking a risk or embracing something new and trusting that all will fall into place as it should. It involves embracing uncertainty, not fearing it. There is no human that can do their job with no uncertainty or risk involved. Surrender is how we gain the confidence to progress.

3 - Delegation

As I talked about in the Non-Stealing section, delegation was scary for me as a new leader. Why is my performance based on the performance of someone else? I can't control it if they screw up. How am I supposed to take ownership of someone else's actions?

I learned that delegation is key to achieving a large plate of tasks and projects beyond my own individual capabilities. Delegating according to strengths is an important skill to have. However, I also learned that no one will do it exactly as you would do it. Expect it. Though we can control aspects of our team's work as the leader, such as what work is delegated to whom and what results are sent out to people beyond our team, we must often surrender to how others execute their work. I had to learn to embrace this rather than resist it. They are not you, so they will not do it exactly as you would. They will do it in their own way and though guidance is important, you must release some control and embrace their differences in order to allow them and the team to progress. Teams are amazing because things can be achieved that we could never achieve on our own.

Control is like a muscle; sometimes we get used to flexing the muscle too tightly and in the wrong situations. We burn valuable energy in situations where we have little control. This does not result in anything fruitful because no matter how hard we flex it, we don't have ultimate control over moving the mountain or shifting the result. By micromanaging we also keep others from learning. Other times, flexing the muscle in subtle ways does wonders for moving ourselves and our teams toward new potential. Like, for example, when we take the opportunity to use an open hour to train a team member on something new or to give them feedback.

In the case of leadership, Surrender is such a critical practice because we don't have control over other humans. You can lead by example but only they can fully engage and receive what you offer. We have control over how we show up, lead by example, offer to teach and participate. Practicing Non-Attachment and Surrender protects our focus, energy, and peace of mind.

◆ ◆ ◆

All in Balance || Surrender

Just like Non-Attachment, Surrender could lead us to be too passive. If we let go of something like our job and sit around waiting for a sign or invitation, this is not Surrender. Surrender involves seeking, inquiry, and embracing opportunity. We must take action. Not everything that is offered has to be integrated into our lives or accepted, but in order to progress and transform, we do have to make the ultimate decision and take action.

The world is big and constantly changing. We, as humans, are also constantly evolving and changing especially early on in our careers. It's important to stay open to possibilities but also to not surrender too soon. We have to have the discipline to follow through on things to really hone our skills and gain depth in areas of our experience. Balancing Surrender with Discipline, by developing a point of view and taking action in responding and moving forward is important. Many of us can get so overwhelmed by the number of options we have that we stop in our tracks and want someone else to choose for us. This approach isn't sustainable and it is not a great practice of Discipline and Self-Study. It's important for you, as an Awake leader, to develop your own relationship and way of collaborating with the universe. The universe never forces you in a direction, though sometimes it may feel like it. It presents the best option and it's up to you to see it and live out that option. When we practice Surrender, we let go of what does not serve us and open up to more possibilities than a limited path that we've accepted or drawn out. You'd be surprised how often the universe and your heart agree.

How do you balance the need for control with the reality of Surrender?

_____

_____

_____

_____

When something doesn't go as planned, how do you respond?

_____

_____

_____

_____

Is there a time when something didn't go as planned but turned out better than expected? Why? What unexpected things came up and how did you respond?

_____

_____

_____

_____

Action

Exercise 1: Something New Each Week

Why? Changing up routines and doing something new is the first step for bringing new opportunities into your work and life.

This exercise is about seeking out new activities, opportunities, knowledge, and people.

If you want to open to new possibility then you must engage in something new and allow the rest to follow. You never know what possibilities and connections will arise when you have an open mind and take the first step in doing something new. Surrender to new possibility by taking the first step and allowing what follows to surprise you.

Here are some Surrender starters:

◆ *Meet someone new for coffee or lunch*

◆ *Sign up for a new fitness class*

◆ *Apply for a new volunteer opportunity or interview for a new job*

◆ *Travel somewhere new alone or join a group travel trip*

◆ *Try a different coffee shop or movie theatre than you're used to*

◆ *Take a different route than you're used to*

◆ *Say "Yes" to something you normally would say "No" to*

Action

Exercise 1: Something New Each Week

What are your favorite ways to discover new opportunities?

_____

_____

_____

_____

What will you try this week that is new?

_____

_____

_____

_____

Let go of things that you often stress over and relentlessly try to control. Make space for more limitless possibility beyond expectations.

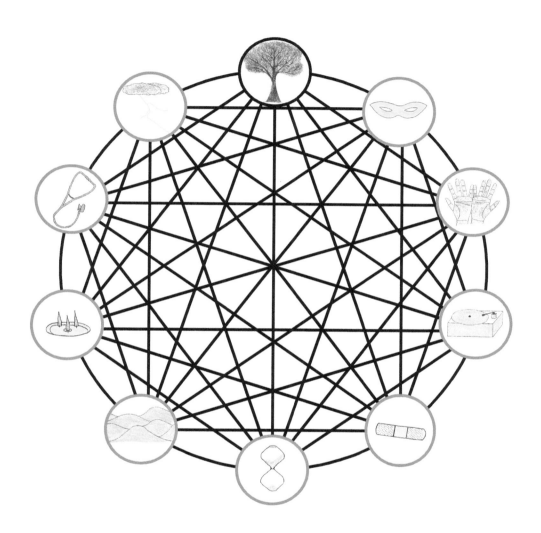

Principle 10

More Good
than Harm

More Good than Harm

You made it to the tenth and final principle! This principle challenges us because we must synthesize everything we have done so far. In our day-to-day actions, no ethical principle is used in a silo. As we can see from the mandala at the end of each section, everything is connected.

Doing More Good than Harm is harder than ever in our very complex, modern business environment. What is the most good? What actually does harm? Sometimes we know we're doing something helpful and good but it also has some negative implications, too. Do you ever feel as though there is a contradiction between the good and harm in your actions? How do we proceed?

In the ancient system, this principle is interpreted as non-violence or non-harming. This seems like an obvious ethical practice; however, even this simple idea of non-harming is not understood or practiced by many people. As leaders, I believe we can all agree that it is not ethical to work toward solutions that harm the earth, the world, our team, or ourselves in the process, even if there are some positive impacts along the way. In the Awake Ethics system, this principle goes beyond just physical harming and into the realm of working toward reducing our harmful impacts on the world, our teams, and ourselves.

To practice More Good than Harm, we put all the other nine principles into play. If you think about it, practicing the other nine principles enables you to do the most good in any given situation. When we maximize the good that we do, we work toward our highest potential. Isn't our highest potential when we're making our most positive impact on the world around us and when we feel at our best? It sounds simple but it is actually very challenging.

In the Stories from the Field, we'll explore how this seemingly simple ethical principle is often lost amongst the fast-paced actions of our business environments.

◆ ◆ ◆

Stories from the Field

1 - The Work We Do

Have you ever felt like you are working hard and following a successful path but don't feel as though your work is fulfilling? Are you skeptical about the positive impacts of your work? Do you ever feel like there's something you could be doing or contributing that is both more fulfilling and making a greater positive impact?

When I was in high school, my favorite activity was shopping (surprising, I know). I would look forward to spending Saturday nights at the mall discovering what was new at my favorite stores. I'd return home with bags of treasures to wear and to decorate my room. In college, I followed my passion for fashion and began working at the headquarters of one of my favorite retail companies.

While interning at this retail company, I came across an excellent book called *Over-Dressed* by Elizabeth Cline. The book detailed the impacts of the fast fashion industry; from environmental impacts of manufacturing to human rights and labor conditions. The information she presented in the book was new and interesting to me, yet very shocking. I saw so much of my own shopping behavior in her critical words about the impacts of mass-produced fast fashion. She wrote about the negative impacts on the environment and the harsh working conditions of many people around the world. What? The effects of my shopping behavior that I thought were so innocent were contributing to harmful effects all over the world? How could the thing I thought was the most good for me, my friends, and my family do so much harm to others and to the environment?

At first, I felt sadness and guilt because my childhood fun and favorite past time was harmful. How could this be true when it was what brought me and my best friends together on the weekends and we shared so much joy in the shopping experience?

I did more research and found her points to be true and relevant. The quality of life of the workers I read about and the long-term vitality of the environment seeped deeper into my heart and overpowered my deep-rooted passion for collecting the newest fashion trends each week. I started cleaning my closet frequently and donating clothing. I started looking at the "Made in" label before purchasing products. I bought pieces that I felt were one-of-a-kind and long-lasting instead of challenging myself to see how many things I could buy with the least amount of money. I had changed my personal behavior to the extent I knew how to in order to do the most good. However, I still kept my retail job. I now faced a more difficult ethical dilemma: if the work I do also has negative impacts, do I exit all together? If you know there is harm in what you do but there are also positive effects, do you stop all together? How could I align my actions with my intentions?

After more research, I realized that how this huge industry has been built up is more than I could single-handedly confront and change. As a leader of my life and my work, with a passion for the company but also a strong conviction to be ethical and maximize the worldly good, I was overwhelmed. After a lot of deliberation and studying these ethical principles, I started to apply what I'd learned. My approach to my work changed dramatically. I began suggesting projects to research and model how we could reduce fuel consumption instead of just reduce time to market. I realized that I could still participate at work while changing the system and its impacts with small nudges.

As leaders, we are held to lead by example in doing the most good and least harm in our roles. However, when we work in a large organization, with national or global reach, and many partners and customers are involved, how do we really know that we're doing the most good and least harm? It's really, really difficult to know all the positive and harmful impacts of our work. It's all connected. Companies highlight only the positive aspects of what they do and offer. Even as employees, we're often far removed from being able to know the full spectrum of impacts our work has on the world. There are a lot of moving parts and unknowns to this equation and it can be challenging to truly know. Many people give up or blindly follow the lead of another person doing something that seems successful.

It's even harder to convince ourselves that we can make a difference at all. We're just one person. Why try? When you realize that not changing your behavior is contributing to the system continuing in the wrong direction, the only option is to change. The first step to making change is awareness. Many leaders have resistance to this first step of awareness. Why? Most often because of fear and distraction. *Everything is okay the way it is so why change it? If I try to change it, I may lose my job. I'll have to actually take ownership of something and potentially do extra work to change.* But what is the cost of not moving forward? Without awareness, which is the Awakening, you cannot identify what action will drive impactful change. The second part is action. You must take actions in your own life to make the change and move toward your highest potential. This is why the drive must be from the heart. If you start there, it will have universal reach and impacts. First become aware of the positive and harmful effects of your work. Meaningful action, connection, and progress will follow.

2 - Technological Progress

Technology has a lot of benefits like improving efficiency, ease, and accuracy. Automation and technology tools have become prevalent in our growing, modern business environment. However, technology also has serious drawbacks when implemented in the wrong application, when implemented too quickly, or without thorough thought about the far-reaching, long-term impacts.

When I was a manager, a new peer on the team decided that she was going to reduce the number of team members significantly (to save money) within the next six months by purchasing a new automated payment system. At the time, there were six people managing auditing and payment operations for the department. She determined that at least three of them could be cut or displaced by implementing this new technology tool. The tool would automate bill auditing and processing, which would make results more accurate and of course reduce cost because of the reduction in human work. While at first this sounded like a great solution, I felt uneasy. The people that currently managed the audits and payments didn't know about it yet and I worried about their well-being. Some of the people that managed auditing and payment operations had been in their position for 15 years. What would they do now?

Once the solution was designed and vetted, the leadership team announced that the tool would be implemented and many positions would be cut within the next six months. They assured the team that they would try to find other positions for them within the company. During the following two weeks, multiple members of that team came to my office crying in fear for what was to come after the new system was fully implemented. They were already looking for new jobs inside and outside the company. They feared what would come next.

Being so close to this situation and the people involved challenged me. I had to gain pretty tight control over my emotions. It was hard to hold the fear of other people. The company did assist in finding jobs for some of them but not all. Many left the company and took significantly lower-paying jobs.

The trend of technology growth has become more and more prevalent in our modern business world. So, what can we learn from this story? How can we, as leaders, continue to do the most good as technology grows? I believe that there was more harm than good in the approach to this technology transition. Whenever people are harmed in a situation, it's the wrong solution. Even if people at the top of the organization will make more money and more high-priced clothing will be available on the market, the solution is never to harm people in the process by abandoning long-standing team members. Customers wouldn't want that either. However, the company decided that more good was to save money and increase efficiency rather than supporting people.

People of all ages join organizations to be supported, to contribute but also to have community and to learn. This speaks to the importance of continuously educating and developing your team members. Leaders must encourage team members to keep learning and also provide them with opportunities to do so. We must identify and give them opportunities to obtain new skills and to continue to learn new ways of thinking and learning. This helps us and our organization as much as it helps them to progress and respond when change happens. This relates back to Non-Stealing and Non-Attachment as forms of doing More Good than Harm. Develop new positions, provide education further upstream, and involve them in other value-adding special projects until they are supported in finding a new job.

As leaders, we must take responsibility for not just our work but also our team members. Competition is tough. Other firms are following the norm and implementing lower-cost solutions that don't involve human labor. This pressures others to do the same to compete, causing a domino effect. However, I challenge you to differentiate. When you take the human aspects away from the business, what is left? Efficiency? Machines? You can choose how you design the inside of your team and organization to make it the best it can be in your eyes. Truly doing the most good will reflect inside and out. If your organization shines inside, it will likely shine outside as well.

A key takeaway here is that even though a tool has many good applications, we can't extrapolate that to conclude that any application we give it is a good application with a positive impact. All tools have good and harmful applications and impacts that are possible. It takes keen observers, healthy skeptics, and heartful leaders to see what applications truly do the most good versus harm. Leaders have the power and responsibility to practice discernment and not just follow the hype or the norm.

3 - Hiring and Firing

In this story, I was on the other side of the table. As leaders, a key responsibility is building and maintaining a strong team. Sometimes we have to make difficult decisions in determining how to make our team stronger and leaner, while still considering the personal human aspects of the situation at large. Ethics are tools for people-centric decision-making.

Another challenging time in my leadership experience was the first time I had to determine whether or not we needed to fire a team member. This team member was working on his personal start-up business during our work hours at the office and was not completing his work for our team on time. He became very careless. His behavior started to affect the quality of our work as a team and the pace at which we were able to progress toward our objectives. There were some aspects of what he did that were still helpful and I didn't have time to take on those ongoing, weekly tedious tasks myself or delegate them to another team member. The team really liked him as a person, too. I spoke with him about the issues I was seeing. I told him that he was keeping the team from progressing and that we needed him to focus and step it up. He listened. However, a week later the same issues began again. What was the most good I could do for the business, the team, myself, and this team member? How long should I hold on?

I attempted to look at what was ethical. Of course I thought back to my experience in the technology situation from Story II. Was I the mean employer firing someone and leaving them high and dry? How did this situation differ? I realized that this team member needed an ethical education more than anything. I had shared with him that he was keeping the team from progressing - from reaching our highest potential - but this did not ultimately change his mindset and his behavior. He needed to learn via experience what I meant. While the people in Story II were giving it their all and loyal devotion, this team member was supported in moving toward his potential but he was not giving back by helping our team accomplish our objectives and reach our highest potential. He was not practicing Truthfulness or Control of Energy. I resolved that letting him go was best for all involved. By letting him go, I would make him aware of his unethical behavior and he would be free to work on his start-up. We could find a team member that would help us move forward. We needed to practice Non-Attachment in order to do the most good. When I approached the situation from an ethical perspective and used this ethical system for guidance, the best decision became clear.

We are often told, as leaders within organizations, that we should do what is best for the business and that we shouldn't let personal feelings affect decisions. However, let's be real: it's all connected. No matter how much we try to separate business and life, at our core, we don't aim to inflict harm on anyone. There are deeply human aspects of business and this is a key difference between serving as a leader and as a team member. Sometimes the truly ethical answer doesn't maximize revenue or drive profit right away. It's a challenge to zoom out and think in terms of what is the optimal solution for everyone involved. It seems there is always a winner and a loser. However, I beg to differ. I believe that there is a more optimal, aligned solution: doing the most good for all involved to lead the individuals and collective toward higher potential. When your energy can collectively work together, great. When you need to work in different directions, allow it and agree to part peacefully.

4 - True Nature

Where I live in California, there is a beautiful tree preserved in the middle of a residential road. When I first passed by this particular road and saw the massive tree standing in the middle of the paved street with a boundary around it, I did a double take. What is that? A construction site? I walked closer. I saw that, no, the tree was indeed preserved in the center of the road, encased by a perimeter container. *How funny*, I thought. I had never seen anything like this. There are often trees planted in sidewalks along the road but I had never seen a huge tree preserved in the center of a well-used residential paved road. I stood and watched as the cars passed beside it on the road, amused and also humbled.

When I think about stories like implementation of technology or firing someone, I always think of this tree. They could have cut it down to build the road. They could have not built that road and preserved the tree. However, they managed to do both. They maximized the good action and minimized the harm. The need for the road was there but the tree was an important existing part of the environment. Whenever I go to get my coffee locally near that spot, I walk by the tree. It's one of my favorite things about that small town in Marin (a close tie with the swing set in the public park). This tree reminds me that there doesn't always have to be a winner and a loser to build and progress. It takes truly passionate, creative leaders to design new solutions that offer the most good. This is the ultimate test of strength and innovation.

Why crush something if you can minimize the harm and even create more good for people and the environment? People often opt for the easy way out or the easy solution, not the Awake solution. The tree symbolizes the people that were let go in Story 2. Had they been developed, given training, and opportunity to contribute in some other way, they could have been productive, valuable parts of the company. Had the leadership detached from their ways, they could have been more creative and open-minded to devise a new solution that offered the most good for all involved.

This all may sound idealistic. I'm not saying it's possible in every case to have such an optimal, happy ending with a clear blue sky where harm is truly zero. As in my story about the fast-fashion realization, change takes time. We have to prioritize. However, I urge you as Awake, aware leaders to pause and think about the impacts on all stakeholders when making decisions and choosing how to lead by example. To be an Awake leader, you must have the bravery, curiosity, and discipline to become aware of the impacts of your actions. By harming someone, you are likely harming or shorting the whole as well as yourself. It's a lot about how you want to spend your time, the legacy you want to leave, and the impact you want to have.

The tree is an example of more good than harm. It shows we're all connected. We benefit from the road and we benefit from the beautiful, healthy tree. To me, it's a symbol of values of the community as well. In Marin, nature is so highly valued and that is why I love it here.

◆ ◆ ◆

All in Balance || More Good than Harm

When we take More Good than Harm too far, we deny our humanness. If we suddenly limit ourselves from doing any harm at all, we feel as though no action at all is maybe the best option. However, we must take action in order to live and to respond to change, which is a constant aspect of our reality.

When I finished reading *Over Dressed*, I thought that I should go become a monk in a far away eco-friendly monastery and have minimal or no impact on the world. I thought it would be better to have no impact than to continue the devastation I was causing by using resources and engaging in work that was apparently harming people. However, I realized that it does not have to be all or nothing. There's nothing wrong with becoming a monk in a monastery. That is one solution. I resolved that I love business because it enables us to learn in a live environment and we connect with people over cool projects, shared efforts, and commerce. There is some good in it. Just like people, there are good and harmful aspects of everything. There are good and harmful applications for all tools and resources. We can only do our best to continuously work in real time to maximize the good effects through our actions. These actions toward More Good than Harm are the ten principles.

Sometimes it's hard to keep up with the change and growing complexity of our actions. It often feels like ignorance is bliss and we should just give in to the spider web of exchanges and routines society has built and conditioned us to believe is the most good. However, when we come across or seek out knowledge and the truth through awareness and experience, our human experience deepens. We're inspired to change for the most good and have discovered a core truth. When we change, we make change. We transform and learn by working through the challenges to find what we truly know and deeply believe is the most good.

Do you ever feel as though there is contradiction between the good and the harmful effects of your work?

_____

_____

_____

_____

Is there a leader or influencer you follow that is especially mindful of doing the most good and least harm?

_____

_____

_____

_____

What company or organization do you respect for doing More Good than Harm? Why do you believe they are doing the most good? Do they do any harm that you know of? Think on all levels: their service to you, others, and the world...

_____

_____

_____

_____

Action

Exercise 1: Impact Chart

Why? Unlayering our actions to understand the true impacts on all levels reveals the true alignment of goodness (or not) in our actions.

In this exercise, we'll begin to bring awareness to the impact of our actions, starting with ourselves. We are most familiar and aware of the impacts of our actions that manifest closest to us. However, as we discussed in Story 1, our actions have impacts far beyond our immediate experience and action, especially in large organizations and businesses.

On the following pages, reflect on and write down what comes to mind when you consider the positive and harmful effects of your work. The goal here is not to over obsess or feel bad about yourself, but to zoom out and think about what you do on a larger scale and how this affects the peace and progress of the world, your organization, your team, your friends and family, and yourself. For each prompt, think of the good and harmful impacts in terms of physical, mental, and emotional impacts. As a challenge, try to balance present impacts with future impacts and relate them, if possible. If you need more space than what I have provided, use a journal or additional space.

Exercise 1: Impact Chart

Question 1: How does the work I do impact the world?

Positive Effects:

Harmful Effects:

Action

Exercise 1: Impact Chart

Question 2: How does the work I do impact my organization?

Positive Effects:

Harmful Effects:

Exercise 1: Impact Chart

Question 3: How does the work I do impact my team members?

Positive Effects:

```



```

Harmful Effects:

```



```

Action

Exercise 1: Impact Chart

Question 4: How does the work I do impact my family and friends?

Positive Effects:

Harmful Effects:

Exercise 1: Impact Chart

Question 5: How does the work I do impact myself?

Positive Effects:

Harmful Effects:

Action

Exercise 1: Impact Chart

Summarizing

On the following page, summarize your answers to the five prompts.

After you have completed the summary page, consider the major takeaways. Which of the positive effects are aligned in driving peace for all the stakeholders including yourself? Which of the positive effects are driving progress? How are the negative effects inhibiting peace and progress from happening?

Action: Using the Principles

How can you work to minimize or eliminate the harm caused? This question can be difficult but you can look to the ten principles for answers. Which of the ten principles could you employ to mitigate or eliminate the harm and allow more positivity to emerge? The other 9 principles are really tools for thinking about this and finding what the root cause of harm is to then resolve it through ethical actions.

Iterate

It's interesting to do this exercise annually as a self-reflection. By bringing awareness to things that are so important and get lost in the day-to-day action mode, we are able to zoom out, see the big important things, and redirect our action toward the most good. A pause and perspective shift can enable us to progress toward our highest potential.

Positive Effects	Harmful Effects
The world:	The world:
The organization:	The organization:
The team:	The team:
Friends and Family:	Friends and Family:
Myself:	Myself:

To do the most good and least harm, start with your own actions. Start with yourself because the ultimate control we have is the ability to lead by example in how we behave, consume, and give.

Maximize the good. Minimize the harm. Seek out your highest potential and support others in doing the same.

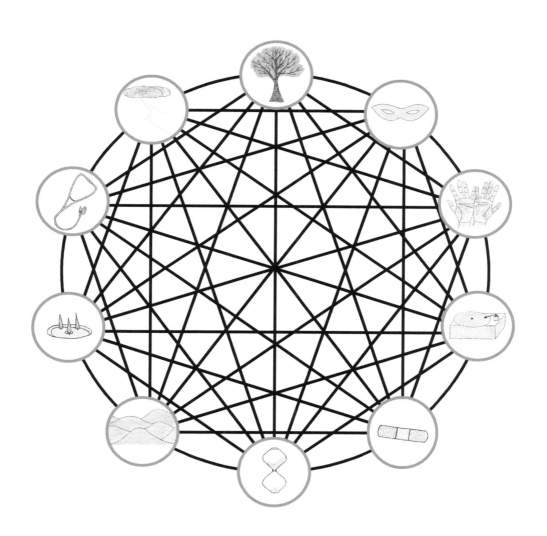

Living the Principles

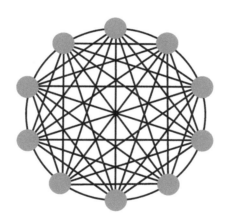

Living the Awake Ethics Principles

Congratulations on making it through all ten sections! This is not easy work. I hope that by now you have found (and have seen many, many times through examples) that our system of ethics guides our decisions day-to-day, helps us align, and connects us with the true intentions and motivation for the work we do. You have seen examples from the field that demonstrate how satisfying progress is driven by human-centered actions. The ten principles guide us as to what human-centered, ethical actions are in any given situation.

You may be asking: If business is a human-made system, then why do we need to study and revisit ethics and human-centered actions? How does business, or action with a goal of profit for humans, not always drive human-centered actions? Business actions, or actions in the interest of profit, are sometimes not in the best interest of the whole. They are often in the best interest of one person while another's wellness or progress is jeopardized. We compromise the overall most good (or optimal most good in balance) to maximize the good for just one person or party, far beyond what is necessary or healthy. This often happens when we just maximize the profit and not the most good. There are so many things we derive good from that cannot translate into money and should not. Some businesses are now measuring progress based on other things like environmental impact, however, it is hard to measure most good on a human level. I don't think it needs one metric. I believe it is shown through a mix of culture, retention, and profit.

You may also be asking: What is my highest potential? What is the highest potential for my team and the world? You may have to read this book 100 times and many other books before having answers to these questions. More importantly, you'll need experience paired with observation and reflection to learn how to maximize the good in any given situation. These are big concepts. Here are three reminders for continuing to move forward toward the answers each day.

The first tip: start by practicing and reflecting on the ten ethical principles in action. Practice the principles and the answer to What is my highest potential? will come. Don't only read, think, and talk about ethics but get out into the world. Work and gain experience in using them in practice. I provide exercises so you can start living the principles day-to-day and integrating them into your work. Think about how each action you take and decision you face as a leader relate to one or more principles and how you can use the principles to inform your decisions and actions. Keep your own ethical diary in your daily pages.

The second tip: continue to return and reflect on the intentions of peace and progress. What is peace? What is progress? Leaders that go through the motions and act without awareness and intention take much, much longer to come into alignment and shape the world in truly good ways. They lose track of why they are doing everything they do. They develop a very narrow, limited focus for their career and their life. Your highest potential is constantly changing, as it is for the world, so it's crucial to come back to this intention day-to-day with each decision you make. I can't tell you what your highest potential is or give you concrete actions to take toward your highest potential because, as we saw throughout the book, the next right action is dependent on so many factors. This ethical system gives us a common language for resolving ethical blind spots and issues more clearly and openly.

Finally, the third tip: remember that we all get off track sometimes. Have you seen people at work and in life fall off the path of ethical, moral correctness? What causes it? Many of the topics we discussed in the guidebook like ego, conditioning, and fear cause us to get off track. However, the primary reason is that these lost individuals don't understand what the most good means. They fall into the system, unaware of the impacts of their actions. This is why, in the book, I offer explanations and examples from experience to illustrate ethics in practice and you reflected on your own leadership practice. The reflections are for awareness. As leaders, we must strive for the advanced skill of holding ourselves accountable for keeping our behavior,

The Awake Ethics Principles

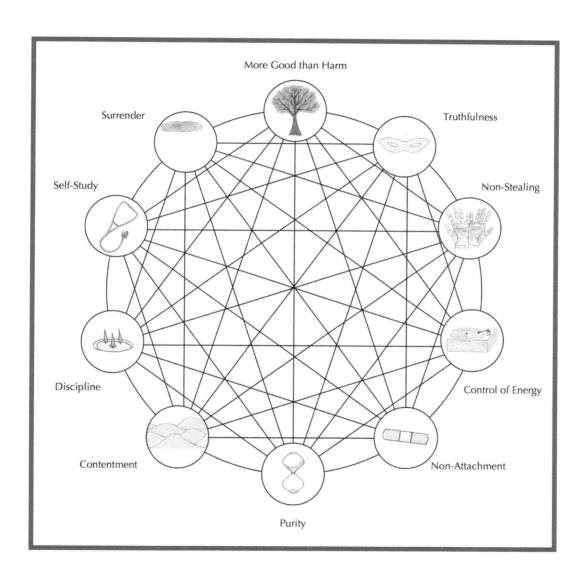

organizations, and systems human-centric. We do this through reflection and tools (like a book or our own support system) for checking ourselves. We must become passionate about staying the course and practice Discipline and Surrender fueled by genuine motivation and curiosity. We hold space and act as a mirror for others, like our team, for staying the course as well. It's a constant, iterative practice as life unfolds. The given events of the day will determine which ethical principles we must apply and practice. It's not a linear thing or a cycle that follows a repetitive pattern except for the cycle of action and reflection.

Continuing to Apply the Principles

Now that you have read this book, you may find that you have become very analytical about your own behavior as well as the behavior of others. How will you deal with those people you encounter that have not read this book and are not so ethical and aware of their actions? How will you collaborate with people who do not have clear intentions of cultivating peace, progress, and moving toward the highest potential? The truth is, I have found, that all people do have this intention deep down; however, it gets buried under a lot of things. As I mentioned, ego, conditioning, and fear are big obstacles to practicing ethics. I will provide a few ways to collaborate in challenging ethical situations and spread these practices of ethics so your organization becomes more peaceful and progressive.

Try out these approaches to action in the field as you go back to work with this new tool belt of ethical knowledge.

1. Lead by example. Don't allow others who act unethically to affect your approach. These individuals need to gradually awaken and that is what Awake leaders help others to do kindly, lovingly, and persistently. We primarily do this just by leading by example but also by giving honest feedback and taking action. Sometimes this is difficult when someone on the team is not being truthful or transparent. It's hard to take the right action rather than the easy or habitual action. However, you now have the tool belt to deal with this situation! As we spoke about, action is better than non-action. You can have a point of view and make progress while still maintaining peace. If you find that your leader is unethical, have a candid conversation to align or go somewhere where you are treated ethically and can lead by example. Don't wait too long.

2. Teach. Use my Stories from the Field as examples as well as the exercises you have practiced and apply the principles to each new situation. These principles are tools: tools for moving toward a more peaceful and progressive workplace. Some days you may need to reflect on them more than others to determine which principles to employ. You are fortunate to have a live environment to practice using these tools. You can teach your team by choosing one principle each week or month to focus on. Spend 30 minutes talking about the principle and gather their feedback and examples of the principle in practice. Share both good examples and examples where better ethical action could have been taken.

3. Be patient. Some days you may need to take rest and time alone to reflect. As you practice more and more, it will get easier to know what decisions and actions are truly ethical. You'll feel more confident. Others will respect you and trust you.

4. Share. You can share this book with your friends, family, and co-workers. If your organization has a leadership program or development program, this book is a good resource to add to it. As more people appreciate and align around modern leadership ethics, it will become more effortless to collaborate and fewer of those tricky situations will arise.

As you progress in your leadership and ethical understanding, the principles and exercises that resonate with you will change and that is normal. Some may not seem relevant to you today but you may encounter someone or a situation in the future where that principle, that story, or that exercise helps you through it and gives you a different perspective to consider. With each day, we add valuable experience to our tool belt. No action and no day of work is wasted if you go into it with a positive intention to move further toward your highest potential with your team and have genuine connection with yourself and others.

To conclude our journey together, I want to thank you for reading and being open to learning. My hope is that you enjoy reflecting on the universal nature of this system and begin to employ the principles in your day-to-day work. I will leave you with one more exercise to begin thinking about how you'll continue to practice the principles. I hope you return to this guide again and again for decision-making and collaboration best practices as you progress and move toward your highest potential.

Preparing to Apply the Principles

Today's Date: _____

The principle that resonated with me as most relevant to focus on now for myself:

_____

_____

_____

Three exercises I'm going to do myself this month:

_____

_____

_____

The principle that resonated with me as most relevant to focus on now with my team:

_____

_____

_____

Three exercises I'm going to practice with my team this month:

_____

_____

_____

Author's Notes

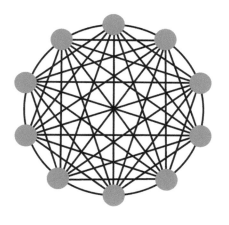

The Pace

A Guide for Working through Awake Ethics

The sample schedule below gives you some guidance for how to work through the book.

Part I: Introduction	→ Week 1
Truthfulness	→ Week 2
Non-Stealing	→ Week 3
Control of Energy	→ Week 4
Reflect, Practice, Observe	→ Week 5
Non-Attachment	→ Week 6
Purity	→ Week 7
Contentment	→ Week 8
Reflect, Practice, Observe	→ Week 9
Discipline	→ Week 10
Self-Study	→ Week 11
Surrender	→ Week 12
Reflect, Practice, Observe	→ Week 13
More Good than Harm	→ Week 14
Part III: Living the Principles	→ Week 15

Note:
I did not put this schedule in the Introduction because every leader has their own pace to work through the book. Feel free to move through it at the pace you like. At different times, different sections and exercises will resonate with you.

Team Exercises Summary

Need a hint? Where should you start? Here are some of the best starter exercises to do as a team:

◆ Field Notes, page 21

◆ Icebreakers, page 24

◆ Team Brainstorm, page 65

◆ Soji, page 80

◆ Wins and Wisdom, page 97 - 98

Best starters for team discussion topics:

◆ Written Communications, page 51

◆ Time Management, page 83

◆ Team Meetings, page 49

On Illustrating

Just like sharing my writing for the first time when I published *Awake Leadership*, I was pretty hesitant to share my own illustrations in this second guidebook. I thought about using photos, clip art, or asking someone to illustrate for me. However, in the spirit of continuous growth and development, I wanted to learn a new skill while writing this book. Writing for me is about the process, and now creating books is about the process, too. It came about naturally that illustrations could more clearly communicate the points I needed to make about ethics.

So much of what I do in my more creative work is rich with metaphor. I always find that metaphor is how we relate seemingly disparate phenomena and relate to each other through practice and story.

One aspect of eastern philosophy that I love is that there is almost always a metaphor provided, usually something in nature. That is what I aim to do with the illustrations, too. Illustrations are rich with metaphor. Even if you have not had an experience yet in leadership similar to my stories, you can hopefully understand the importance and truth to the principles based on the illustrative example and metaphor.

It was a big decision to print the book fully in color, with so much color. However, shedding light on each principle is what I aim to do section by section and the color contrast is key for showing the progression throughout the book.

While illustrating, I found that it works best when you don't start with the details, but start with the big picture: the shape and the basic components. Get the basic components on the page first. Zoom out first to get the big picture and the details will become clear and fall into place.

When you find something that you truly enjoy - the process as well as the result - it's so incredibly satisfying.

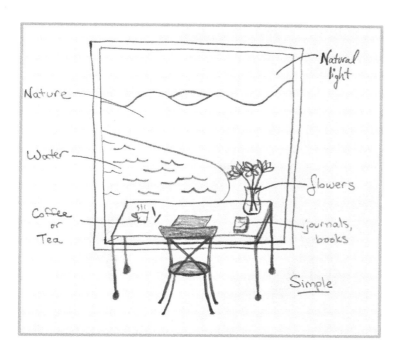

My Ideal Environment Example from Purity Exercise 2.

This is where most of this book was written!

The Ancient System

The system of ethics I present in the guidebook is based on an ancient system that originated in India. This system of moral conduct, comprised of ten ethical principles, provided me with a foundation upon which to guide my own behavior and decision-making in my leadership practice at work and in my own life. However, I saw that many people couldn't easily apply it in their own modern lives because it needed to be reiterated through a modern lens. I don't believe in reinventing the wheel when something works so well and is tried and true, but I do believe in updating systems to make them relevant, relatable, and applicable for a modern audience.

The system is based on millennia of experience, not just my own. It has helped me to vastly improve my standard of work and living. It has helped me to move further toward what I feel is my own highest potential as a leader. The system has helped me achieve balance, alignment, and strength in my leadership of my work and my life. Studying this system and systems from other cultures and time periods has opened my eyes to the universality of the human experience across cultures.

The Yamas and Niyamas are the first two limbs of the eight-limbs of yoga as written in the Yoga Sutra by Patanjali. The Yamas are comprised of five ethical disciplines of conduct toward others. The Niyamas are comprised of five moral principles to practice toward ourselves.

The Ancient System

Yamas	Niyamas
Practices toward others.	Practices toward ourselves.
1. *Ahimsa* - Non-Harming	1. *Saucha* - Purity
2. *Satya* - Truth	2. *Santosa* - Contentment
3. *Asteya* - Non-Stealing	3. *Tapas* - Discipline
4. *Brahmacharya* - Self-restraint	4. *Svadhyaya* - Self-Study
5. *Aparigraha* - Non-Attachment	5. *Isvara pranidhana* - Surrender

Further reading on the traditional Yamas and Niyamas:

◆ Light on Yoga by B.K.S. Iyengar, pages 31 - 40

◆ The Yoga Sutras of Patanjali by Sri Swami Satchidananda

Thank You Notes

Thanks first and foremost to the Awake Leadership readers. Your kind words of support, gratitude, and encouragement brought this second book to life! It's true.

Thanks to my team of helpers that diligently gave feedback along the way and offered excellent editing guidance. You are key in bringing my vision to reality.

Thanks to my teachers and leaders for sharing your wisdom and giving me experience and opportunities.

About Hilary

Hilary Jane Grosskopf is a leadership guide, strategist, and writer. Her writing is inspired by her experience as a leader in a variety of organizations and her study of systems. As Founder of Awake Leadership Solutions, she helps leaders to develop strong leadership skills, build the teams of their dreams, and achieve bold objectives.

awakeleadershipsolutions.com

Also by Hilary

Awake Leadership
A system for leading with clarity and creativity.

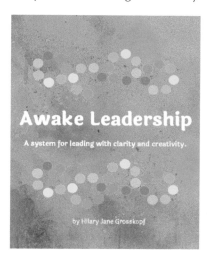

Awake Leadership is a system of seven vitals for successful leadership in action. While many leadership books detail qualities of excellent leaders, this guide shows how to lead through a progression of specific practices. Each section of the guidebook contains interactive exercises with examples and tips for putting the vitals into action. Learn practices for aligning and motivating your team. Achieve your collective and individual goals with more enthusiasm and ease.

Available on Amazon.com.

Learn more at awakeleadershipsolutions.com.

Awake Ethics

CPSIA information can be obtained
at www.ICGtesting.com
Printed in the USA
LVHW071030220819
628522LV00001B/2/P

9 781732 358300